Shining Glory

Shining Glory

Theological Reflections on Terrence Malick's *The Tree of Life*

Peter J. Leithart

CASCADE *Books* · Eugene, Oregon

SHINING GLORY
Theological Reflections on Terrence Malick's *The Tree of Life*

Cascade Books
An Imprint of Wipf and Stock Publishers
199 W. 8th Ave., Suite 3
Eugene, OR 97401

www.wipfandstock.com

ISBN 13: 978-1-62032-413-4

Cataloguing-in-Publication data:

Leithart, Peter J.

    Shining glory : theological reflections on Terrence Malick's *The Tree of Life* / Peter J. Leithart.

    x + 88 pp. ; 23 cm.

    ISBN 13: 978-1-62032-413-4

    1. Malick, Terrence, 1945– —Criticism and interpretation. 2. Motion Pictures—Religious aspects. I. Title.

PN1998.3 M3388 L50 2013

Manufactured in the U.S.A.

Contents

Preface

I HAD READ SOME of the critics on Terrence Malick's *The Tree of Life* before I saw it with family members in Atlanta two years ago, but nothing prepared me for the experience of watching the movie. I was enthralled from the first moments. I had known the O'Briens for all of five minutes when I saw Mrs. O'Brien receive news of her son's death by telegram and Mr. O'Brien receive the news over the phone, but I had to hold back tears. How did Malick do that? How did he make me care so much so quickly? It was one of the most beautiful films I had ever seen, drenched in prayer, shot-through with the biggest questions that we humans pose about our lives and our world, more philosophically and theologically sophisticated than any film I knew. I was an instant fan, and as I have watched it again and again since I have grown to love and admire it all the more. A friend commented to me after another viewing that Malick did things in this film that he had always hoped to see in movies. It's not unprecedented, I know, but it is rare enough to be nearly in a class of its own. *The Tree of Life* is not just another film, but another way of doing film.

One commentator says that there is an "idea in every shot," but I think that is an understatement. There are more ideas in the film than there are minutes, and despite their range and complexity they form a coherent whole. It's not a coherent whole that I entirely agree with. I am skeptical about the evolutionary portrait of origins that Malick depicts, even more skeptical about Malick's too-easy conflation of biological and biblical themes. I think the critics who call Malick a dualist and a Gnostic are wrong, but they aren't insane. I offer a defense of the "eternity" scenes at the end, but I agree that they aren't the full-blooded scenes of consummation that Christians hope for.

My purpose in this essay, however, is not to critique and argue but to understand both what the film means and *how* it means. Inevitably, I have tried to understand the film with my own brain and using the disheveled piles of ideas I've stored in there over the years. I watch a fair number of movies, but I am not a film scholar. I watched the film as a theologian whose main work has been in biblical theology, and so I'm naturally drawn to the biblical melodies and chords that echo throughout. That makes my interpretation one-sided and perhaps idiosyncratic, but I have attempted to watch carefully enough to honor the filmmaker's intentions. I do not expect a great deal of biblical knowledge from the reader, but I do assume that the reader has seen the film. I describe a few scenes in detail, but I refer to many scenes briefly because I wrote for a reader familiar enough with the movie to know what I'm talking about. If you haven't seen *The Tree of Life*, do so before reading. Better yet, watch it three times. Then listen to the sound track, and watch it again.

If at that point you still need the book, it will be here waiting.

Acknowledgments

I BENEFITTED FROM CONVERSATIONS with a number of people about *The Tree of Life*. James Jordan showed the film at the 2012 Biblical Horizons Summer Conference, and the ensuing discussion was enormously helpful to me. Observations from Jeff Meyers and Toby Sumpter were particularly insightful. David Hart offered more information about Terrence Malick than I had been able to find anywhere else and I was gratified to find that David shared my enthusiasm for the film. I learned much from watching the film with Joshua Appel and Douglas Jones. A number of my sons, all of whom know more about film than I do, pointed things out that I would not have noticed without them. I am grateful to them all, but especially to Malick and his crew for making such an extraordinary film.

Chapter 1

Visual Lyricism

"Love smiles through everything."

——Mrs. O'Brien

The first time I watched *The Tree of Life* in an Atlanta theater, one of the people with me was so confused by the film that she didn't realize until the credits rolled that Sean Penn and Hunter McCracken were playing the same character at different ages (Jack O'Brien). After the film opened, the story spread that an Italian projectionist got the reels confused and showed the second before the first. Nobody noticed the mistake until it was all over.

Anecdotes such as these tell us something about our expectations of film, and how Terrence Malick's 2010 film violates them. Film is often thought to be a narrative art. That's an understandable perspective. Many films are based on novels, graphic or otherwise, and films share many of the features of a literary narrative—character, setting, episode, a plot with beginning, middle, and end. It's possible to use the categories and concepts of literary criticism to describe film. Films play with temporal sequences, but filmmakers learned that from storytellers, beginning with the Homer of the *Odyssey*.

Whatever we might say about the general run of films, Malick is *not* essentially a narrative filmmaker and *The Tree of Life* is not essentially a narrative film. Anyone who comes to the film with the expectation that its main business is to tell a story is going to lose his way, and is likely to be disappointed.

The Tree of Life is hard to follow. Characters are not always easy to identify,[1] and most are never named. The film makes quick cuts, sometimes to scenes that seem completely unrelated to the previous action. Scenes overlap with and spill into each other, so that at some moments in the film there are three or more time-frames at work simultaneously, one visual, one in voiceover, one indicated by the music. Terms like "elusive," "elliptical," "impressionistic" slip regularly from the critics.[2]

Yet the film does tell a story and, for all its complexities and sophistications, and for all the large questions that it raises, the film's narrative is quite simple. Though not shown in chronological sequence, three main time periods are identifiable by the age of the characters, especially Jack, and by the style of cars and houses. The earliest period, which we glimpse early in the movie but settle into halfway through the film, is the infancy, childhood, and boyhood of the O'Brien boys. Jack's earliest years are given in fragmentary flashbacks that eventually settle into longer episodes. During the longest narrative sequence, Jack is twelve years old. The second period, which we see early in the film, takes place about a decade later. The O'Brien parents are no longer living in their earlier home. We never see Jack or his brother R. L. in this second time period, only Mr. and Mrs. O'Brien. The most recent period is Jack's middle age, when Jack is played by a brooding Sean Penn. Though the first time frame in the film receives the most airtime, the crucial time frame is the last—Jack's adult "present."

The opening of the film introduces us to the categories that we need for making sense of the film. In a voiceover accompanying the opening scenes, Mrs. O'Brien (Jessica Chastain) recalls a lesson that she learned from the nuns concerning the "way of nature" and the "way of grace." We see scenes from her childhood and she is shown as an adult swinging from the tree swing, playing with her boys, sitting at the dinner table with her husband and family. Only a few minutes into the film, Mrs. O'Brien declares her

1. In the scene where a boy drowns in the local swimming pool, we see his hysterical mother bending over him screaming as he is pulled from the pool. She could be Jessica Chastain's sister and she's wearing a print swimsuit similar to Chastain's. She's screaming the boy's name "Tyler," which is not one of the O'Brien boys. Since only Jack's name is spoken in the movie, though, we don't really know if "Tyler" is one of the O'Brien boys or not. For a split second we fear that one of the O'Brien boys has died. Malick no doubt did this deliberately. Because of the boy's drowning, Jack begins to doubt God; he walks away from the tree of life and in a sense dies to innocence because of the death of the drowned boy.

2. See the summary of critical responses to the film in David Hudson, "Cannes 2011: Terrence Malick's *The Tree of Life*," available online at http://mubi.com/notebook/posts/cannes-2011-terrence-malicks-the-tree-of-life.

loyalty to God and the way of grace with the words, "I will be true to you, whatever comes." As we hear "whatever comes," a delivery boy carries a telegram to her front door. It is devastating news, and she collapses with an aborted cry of "O God." Later we learn that her second son, R. L., died at the age of nineteen. R. L.'s death is the heart of the film, the tragic center around which everything else circulates.

We never learn how R. L. died, but that episode fills the entire film with Malick's own anguish. In his 1998 *Vanity Fair* profile of Malick, Peter Biskind wrote of Malick's brothers:

> Larry, the youngest, went to Spain to study with the guitar vir-
> tuoso Segovia. Terry discovered in the summer of 1968 that Larry
> had broken his own hands, seemingly despondent over his lack
> of progress. Emil [Malick's father], concerned, went to Spain and
> returned with Larry's body; it appeared the young man had com-
> mitted suicide. Like most relatives of those who take their own
> lives, Terry must have borne a heavy burden of irrational guilt.
> According to Michèle, the subject of Larry was never mentioned.[3]

The Tree of Life is a cinematic homage to Larry Malick, a celluloid requiem. After the opening sequence, the film focuses on a single day in the life of the adult Jack, which is the anniversary of R. L.'s death. Jack is an architect at a large and prosperous firm, but he is spiritually withered, haunted and guilt-ridden by the memory of his brother. Jack has wandered away from the God he knew as a boy, and now stumbles through a dry and weary land where there is no water. In his mind's eye, he sees R. L. standing at a beach beckoning: "Find me," he says. The rest of the film is Jack's attempt, on this one day, to be restored to his brother, to be reconciled to his brother's fate, and thereby to be reconciled to the universe.

Jack remembers swimming in the Brazos River near Waco and at the local swimming pool. He remembers playing dodge ball in the yard. Above all, he recalls an earlier period of his life when he had wandered away. When a boy drowns in the swimming pool, he questions God's goodness and the order of the universe. Already estranged from his domineering father, Jack withdraws even further, and becomes alienated from his mother and brother as well. When he hurts R. L., his brother refuses to take vengeance. He for-gives Jack and the two are reconciled. R. L.'s compassion touches off recon-ciliations between Jack and his father and mother, as well as with others in

---

3. Peter Biskind, "The Runaway Genius," *Vanity Fair* (1998), page numbers not noted or recalled.

the neighborhood. As Jack recalls those events of his boyhood, he relearns the lesson R. L. taught him. At the end, he finds R. L. on the beach in a vision of reunion that includes not only his brothers but his parents, neighbor children, everyone who has appeared in the film and more. At the end of the day, Jack emerges from his high-rise office building with a relaxed look on his face. He has been reconciled to the cosmos, and his dead brother was the mediator of that reconciliation. The death that drove him away paradoxically brings him back.

To say that the film is not primarily narrative is not to say it lacks incident. As in the novels of Marilynne Robinson (*Gilead, Home*), *The Tree of Life* is stuffed with events, but many are told so obliquely, so briefly, that we barely register that they have happened. When Jack is a toddler, there is a brief scene of Mrs. O'Brien hurriedly carrying Jack across the lawn, her face twisted with terror. Behind her a man lies on the lawn shaking with an epileptic fit as another man bends over him to help. An overturned bicycle is on the lawn nearby. What happened? Who are these men? Did the man recover? We never find out. As Mrs. O'Brien walks through town with her boys, they encounter several criminals being packed away into police cruisers. Mrs. O'Brien gives one of the criminals water from her thermos. The criminals never appear in the film again either. What did they do? Where are they going? These minimalist vignettes are the fragments of a life remembered, a collection of "Remember the time whens?" And they are affecting and effective in the same way that memories are.

Malick is not a dialogue-centered filmmaker either. Minutes pass in *The Tree of Life* without words exchanged between characters, and the voice-over doesn't fill that gap, since most of the voice-over, if it is dialogue at all, is dialogue with God. Set against the background of the film's visuals and music, the voice-overs can be quite moving, but they are portentious and occasionally flirt close to the border of pretention. What dialogue there is tends to be stilted and formal, more symbolic and thematic than dramatic. Characters play thematic and archetypal roles. We learn a good deal about Mr. O'Brien's past, but nothing at all about Mrs. O'Brien's. Mr. O'Brien works in a factory, and invents things. What he invents, we're never quite sure. What realism there is to the characterization is the work of the superb cast as much as the screenplay.[4]

4. Most of the actors, perhaps 75 percent, are non-professionals. The three main adult characters (Mr. and Mrs. O'Brien, and the adult Jack) are played by three of the world's best-known actors—Brad Pitt and Jessica Chastain as the O'Briens and Sean Penn as the adult Jack. They are all excellent. Chastain is ethereal; Penn, who has little to do besides

If *The Tree of Life* were nothing more than this oft-told family story, it would hardly merit so much attention as I am giving it. What makes *The Tree of Life* a masterpiece is Malick's decision to widen the scope of this small family story and his exploitation of the visual poetry of film.

Some viewers are confused by Malick's insertion of a lengthy sequence depicting the evolution of the universe, of earth, and of life. Though it might appear out of place, the sequence fits perfectly with the small family story that Malick tells. The O'Briens suffer a devastating loss, and Malick knows from his own experience that every loss raises global questions about the justice of the world. Everyone who suffers or witnesses inexplicable pain asks, as the O'Briens' pastor does, "Is there some fraud in the universe?" Malick signals that his interest in the problem of suffering is a theological one in the first frame of the film, which contains a quotation from the book of Job. He paints the small family story on a canvas as big as the cosmos. And he paints it in brilliant colors and with a fascinating composition. One critic noted that while most movies have "moments of poetic montage," in this case "the entire film is a poetic montage."[5] The film is gorgeous.

Mrs. O'Brien invites us to see the love shining through everything, and Malick's film not only tells us to see it but makes us see it. *Malick gives the gorgeous surface depth and emotional power by the way he overlaps visuals, music, sounds, voices, characters, and episodes.* The film delivers what it has to deliver through the dense metaphoricity and visual allusion, juxtaposition of images, and the inversion or twisting of normal clock time. The film is itself a tree, "with seeds, roots, trunk, branches, sticks . . . and leaves, all undergoing duress and change under the weight/wait of Time."[6]

brood, broods splendidly; Pitt leaves us with the right mix of hatred, admiration, and pity for his domineering, affectionate father. None of the boys have ever been in a film before *The Tree of Life*. The young Jack, Hunter McCracken, perfectly exhibits the awkwardness and cruel innocence of preadolescence. His hunched shoulders and angular movements exude the self-consciousness that every twelve-year-old feels: "All the world is watching *me*, and I both love and hate the attention." Laramie Eppler as R. L. is sweet and kind in an entirely boyish way, his crooked, impish grin one of the film's most absorbing images. Tye Sheridan as the youngest brother Steve is marginal to the film, but does his work well.

5. Michael Tully, "The Tree of Life—A Hammer to Nail Review," *Filmmaker*, filmmakermagazine.com/24499-the-tree-of-life-a-hammer-to-nail-review. Others have described the film as a "tone poem," and some of the scenes use what experimental filmmaker Thomas Wilfred calls "visual music." See David Cummings, Michael Sicinski, and Kevin Lee, "Secret Experiments in 'The Tree of Life,'" http://www.fandor.com/blog/secret-experiments-in-the-tree-of-life-part-ii-influences-and-antecedents.

6. "Terrence Malick's Song of Himself," http://nilesfilmfiles.blogspot.com/2011/06/song-of-himself-terrence-malicks-tree.html.

Visual allusion first. The allusiveness is so dense and compact that nearly everything in the film is announced in the first moments of the film. The sound of waves and gulls in the first frames takes us forward to the beach scene at the end. A quotation from the book of Job gives the story an epic biblical thrust, and the flame that is the first visual reappears just before the credits. Windows, breezes, grass, nature, grace, beauty, glory, hands, sunflowers, trees, sky—we see or hear about all of these in the first few minutes, and over the course of the film these images recur, spiral out, flower and bloom. Sounds, words, and concepts are linked with visual images, so that when the visual images recur later they carry the concepts along with them. Images get packed with multiple significances. The "tree" of the title is the biblical tree of life, the tree that Mr. O'Brien plans, the backyard tree that the boys climb, the evolutionary tree of Darwinian biology.

Juxtaposition of scenes, and the layered overlap of scenes and dialogue, are crucial techniques for Malick. Early in the film, as Mrs. O'Brien completes her opening meditation on nature and grace, she says "The nuns taught us that no one who lives in the way of grace comes to a bad end." At that moment, the camera closes in on R. L., whose early death appears to be a standing contradiction to the nuns' simple message. In a charming moment early in the second half, we see toddler Jack being led by a mysterious female figure through a forest. Then he is in an underwater bedroom, his teddy bear floating nearby and his crib rising and beginning to overturn. He swims through the door and Malick cuts to Mrs. O'Brien in the final stages of labor. The underwater bedroom is the womb, the swim out of the door is Jack's birth. This juxtaposition sets up visual allusions later on. When Jack is a young teen, a boy drowns in the local swimming pool, and it is as if Jack has passed through a second birth into questioning adulthood. Near the end of the film Mrs. O'Brien swims out a door into a new life. What was initially a figure of birth finally becomes a figure of new birth, resurrection.

One wonderful sequence moves through the following scenes:

- Mrs. O'Brien playfully wakes the boys by touching ice cubes on their feet and stuffing cubes down their shirts.

- She takes them into town, where they encounter some criminals being stuffed into police cars. Mrs. O'Brien pauses to offer a drink of water to one of the men as the boys look on wondering, "Could that happen to anyone?"

- A second cycle begins with Mr. O'Brien waking the boys. The camera is behind and below him, making him a gigantic, shadowy faceless figure as he explodes through the door of their room, roughly pulls back their covers, and gets them out of bed. The contrast with Mrs. O'Brien's playfulness is stark. Mr. O'Brien is also taking the boys on an excursion, to a church or theater where Mr. O'Brien plays Bach's *Toccata and Fugue in D Minor* on the organ. Throughout the following series of scenes, Bach continues to play. Through the following scenes, we are still in the scene at the organ.

- Mr. O'Brien sprays his laughing boys from the garden hose. Bach continues playing.

- Jack slams the screen door, waking Mr. O'Brien from a nap. Mr. O'Brien makes him close the screen door fifty times, quietly. Bach continues playing.

- Mr. O'Brien, his hand heavily on Jack's neck, shows him how to weed the yard. "You have to get at the roots." Bach continues playing.

- Mr. O'Brien plays slap-hands with the boys on the sofa while Mrs. O'Brien looks on smiling. Bach continues playing.

- During the game of slap-hands, we begin to hear the voice of Mr. O'Brien giving life advice to Jack: "Your mother is naïve. It takes fierce will to get ahead in this world. All these top executives, you know how they got where they are? They floated right down the middle of the river." Bach continues playing.

- During his advice, we see Mr. O'Brien leave the house, throwing open the screen door and letting it slam shut. Bach continues playing.

- Mr. O'Brien plays cards, and does not seem to be doing well. In the voice-over, he continues giving his advice. Bach continues playing.

- Mr. O'Brien walks down the street with Jack telling him not to give up on his dreams. He confides that he dreamed of being a concert pianist, but let "life get in the way." Before he knew it, he had lived his life and given up his dream. Bach continues playing.

- As Mr. O'Brien talks, we see a brief glimpse of a barren desert landscape, the landscape that the adult Jack has been wandering through early in the film. Here it doesn't represent Jack's shriveled soul, but the dried up soul of his father. Bach continues playing.

- Then we are back to Mr. O'Brien playing the organ with Jack watching beside him. The whole sequence has been in a sense a single "scene."

- While Mr. O'Brien plays, another voice begins to speak, the voice of the O'Brien's pastor, preaching on the book of Job. The scene changes to a church service, as the *Toccata and Fugue* fades.

At several points in this sequence, three scenes occur at the same time: We watch Mr. O'Brien playing with his boys or at a card game; in a voice-over, he gives advice to his boys about how to get ahead in life, advice that he actually gives during his walk with Jack, which we see only much later in the sequence; meanwhile, the music reminds us that we are still standing with Jack, uncomfortable in suit and tie, watching Mr. O'Brien play the organ. Given the role that music has played in Mr. O'Brien's life, the music that runs through the sequence of scenes is an ongoing reminder of his failed dreams.

The Tree of Life is confusingly arranged, not only in its broad sweep but also in specific episodes. In one scene, Jack watches R. L. paint with water colors. A glass of water sits on the table next to R. L. There is a quick cut to a slamming screen door and Jack screaming at Mrs. O'Brien, "What do you know!? You let him walk all over you!" Mrs. O'Brien goes back to the table, sadly picks up R. L.'s dripping painting, and lets some excess water run off. Only then do we get a hint of what has happened. In actual time, the sequence was: R. L. was painting; Jack turned the glass of water over on his painting; Mrs. O'Brien scolded Jack, who stormed out of the house; and Mrs. O'Brien returned to clean up the mess. In the film the sequence is: R. L. painting, Jack storming out, and Mrs. O'Brien cleaning up the mess. Not only is the film's rendering of the scene out of order, but it leaves out the key moment of the episode, when Jack spoils R. L.'s watercolor. Atemporal sequences like this force temporality into the open as a theme of the film. Much of the film is concerned with the healing of time, as the adult Jack tries to recover contact with boy that he was so that he can become whole.

Malick's thematic breadth and his exploitation of the aesthetic capacities of film put *The Tree of Life* in a class of its own. I have watched Malick's earlier films with appreciation, occasionally with awe, but none comes close to the majesty, beauty, and challenge of *The Tree of Life*. It is, as Michael Tully says, "Malick's magnum opus. It's the film he was born to make."[7] But it's not only Malick's masterpiece. It is one of the great films

7. Michael Tully, "The Tree of Life—A Hammer to Nail Review," *Filmmaker*,

ever made. All the life of everything is here—creation and consummation, birth and death, laughter and tears, success and failure and the failures embedded within success, male and female, sin and shame, trees and
water and sky and sun, distant galaxies and the neighbor's lawn. One of
the purposes of art is to enhance our attention to the world around us,
and by this standard Malick's film is art of the highest order.

filmmakermagazine.com/24499-the-tree-of-life-a-hammer-to-nail-review.

9

Chapter 2

Job

"No one knows when sorrow might visit his house any more than Job did."

— FATHER HAYNES

THE FIRST FRAME OF *The Tree of Life* is a quotation from the biblical book of Job, written in white letters against a black background. There is no music, only the faint lapping of waves and crying of gulls. We are ushered immediately into a biblical world and a biblical story, and into a story of suffering, loss, and death.

Job is about unaccountable suffering. Job is a great man in the land of Uz, who is introduced in the first verse of the book as possessing a fourfold righteousness: "blameless, upright, fearing God, and turning away from evil" (Job 1:1). He is so righteous that he covers the possible sins of his sons by offering sacrifice (1:4–5). Job is also exceedingly wealthy, with flocks and herds and many servants. He is "the greatest of all the men of the east" (1:3).

Job's wealth inspires Satan to present a temptation plan before Yahweh when the sons of God assemble. "Of course Job serves the Lord," Satan says. "The Lord has set him in a cocoon of wealth and power, shielding him from the slings and arrows that are the lot of most men. Who wouldn't be pious under such circumstances? Remove the shield, and see what happens when Job is exposed." The Lord agrees to test whether Job's faithfulness is a *quid* for God's *quo*. In a quick series of four disasters, Job loses his oxen, sheep, camels, servants, and children. A great wind comes at the end, striking the house where his children feast and make the house fall. And great is its fall (1:13–19). Then the Lord allows Satan to strike Job's person, covering him with boils. At the end of it all, Job is left with nothing, sitting in ashes, scraping his boils with a fragment of pottery, bewildered that his life could collapse so completely so quickly (2:8). Despite his wife's urging, Job refuses to curse God, but he does curse the day of his birth: "Let the day perish on which I was to be born, and the night which said, 'A boy is conceived'" (3:2–3).

The bulk of Job consists of lengthy dialogues between Job and his three friends, Eliphaz, Bildad, and Zophar (2:11). They are convinced that Job would not suffer so severely unless he had committed some great sin. Job rejects this assessment of his situation. There is no proportion, he insists, between his suffering and his life. He suffers unjustly, and he longs for the opportunity to appear before the Lord, his Judge, and offer his defense.

After many chapters of fruitless debate, the Lord himself appears in a whirlwind to Job and his friends. Yahweh agrees that Job has spoken rightly about him, unlike the friends (42:7). The bulk of Yahweh's speech is a reminder of his creative power. He laid the foundations of the earth, enclosed the sea, set the stars in the heavens, and gave them their names. Yahweh is the midwife for the mountain goats who give birth, the zookeeper who feeds the wild donkeys and oxen that human beings don't even know. He gave power to the horse, and makes the hawk soar in the sky, and he is even able to guide and control the great monsters, Behemoth and Leviathan.[1]

This has sometimes been read as peevish complaint: "Look here, Job, I'm busy running a big world, and your little problems barely register." That entirely misses the point, but so does the more common, more traditional, suggestion that Yahweh is merely silencing Job by reminding him of his sovereign power. God's speech is a reminder that he cares for his creation, forgets nothing, leaves nothing to chance. Job cannot know all that Yahweh is up to in this great world of his, but the thrust of the speeches is that a God like Yahweh who cares for calving deer will take note of his suffering servant and deliver him from death. Jesus sums up Job's message concisely: "Consider the birds of the air. They neither toil nor spin, yet your heavenly Father feeds them. . . . If He feeds the birds of the air, will He not also feed you, O you of little faith?"

Beyond that, however, the Lord has orchestrated Job's life, including his sufferings, to bring Job into glory.[2] Job is a faithful, blameless man at the outset, but he doesn't yet stand among the sons of God who appear

1. *The Tree of Life* contains a menagerie: Velociraptors, a plesiosaur (Leviathan?), birds, a goldfish, a frog, a lizard. The animals reinforce the Job theme, and also hint at the biblical story of Noah's ark.

2. This is the theme highlighted by Toby Sumpter, *A Son for Glory* (Monroe, LA: Athanasius, 2012).

before Yahweh. He offers sacrifice, but sacrifice is both a drawing-near and a confirmation of distance. Sacrifices are offered by worshipers who stand afar off. After Job passes through the fire of loss and the furnace of his comforters' accusations, he emerges purified and glorified. He stands before the Lord, as he had always hoped, and intercedes for his friends. God comes near to Job to wrestle with him, so that he can make him stronger. God sends windy trials to prepare Job to stand before the whirlwind of God's own presence.

Job doesn't offer a theodicy, a philosophical solution to the problem of evil. Rather, the Book of Job points those who suffer undeservedly to the Creator God and issues a call to faith. Job doesn't answer the problem of undeserved suffering. Its message is relevant precisely in the *absence* of explanations.

Malick opens his film with a quotation from the first part of Yahweh's speech from the whirlwind: "Where were you when I laid the foundation of the earth . . . When the morning stars sang together, and all the sons of God shouted for joy?" (Job 38:4, 7). The quotation signals that the film will be a meditation on suffering and death, and particularly on undeserved suffering and death, and it hints that the film will respond to suffering and evil in the way that Job does—by pointing to the Creator.

Jack O'Brien is the Job of the film, Jack O'Brien, his very name (the only name given in the film) identifying him with the archetypal sufferer.[3] He suffers because of the untimely death of his younger brother. In the opening voice-over, Mrs. O'Brien states the nuns' teaching that those who live in the way of grace never come to a bad end. As she says these words, the camera moves closer to young R. L., the middle O'Brien boy who will die at the age of nineteen. He will come to a bad end, even though he is the best of the O'Brien boys. He is good, brave, kind, faithful, forgiving. He is creative, an artist and a musician. Yet this model of boyhood dies before his prime. For Jack, this can only mean that there is something amiss in the universe. The world is a trap, set up to frustrate hope.

After R. L.'s death, Mrs. O'Brien has to deal with a Job's comforter, her own mother, who assaults Mrs. O'Brien will a series of well-meaning but unfeeling clichés: "You'll get over it. You still have your memories of him. You have to be strong. Time passes, things change, nothing stays the same.

3. See Joe McCulloch, "Terrence Malick's 'The Tree of Life': A Few Thoughts Subsequence to a Local Screening Sponsored by a College's Theology Department," http://mubi.com/notebook/posts/terrence-malicks-the-tree-of-life-a-few-thoughts-subsequent-to-a-local-screening-sponsored-by-a-colleges-theology-department.

The Lord gives and takes away; that's the way he is. He sends flies to wounds that they may heal." Most cuttingly of all, "You still have the other two." Mrs. O'Brien doesn't want to get over it. She responds to the absurdity of her son's death with cries and shrieks, which float disembodied through the treetops that bend in the wind, as if to fill nature with her grief. Emotionally, she is with Job in the ash heap.

In the second half of the film, there is a long scene of a church service. The sermon is on Job, and the pastor goes on at length about the inevitability of suffering.

> Job imagined he might build his nest on high, that the integrity of his behavior would protect him against misfortune. And his friends thought, mistakenly, that the Lord could only have punished him because secretly he'd done something wrong. But no. Misfortune befalls the good as well. We can't protect ourselves against it. We can't protect our children. We can't say to ourselves, "Even if I'm not happy I'm going to make sure they are." We run before the wind. We think that it will carry us forever. It will not. We vanish as a cloud. We wither as the autumn grass and like a tree we are rooted up. Is there some fraud in the scheme of the universe? Is there nothing which is deathless, nothing which does not pass away? We cannot stay where we are. We must journey forth.[4] We must find that which is greater than fortune or fate. Nothing can bring us peace but that. Is the body of the wise man or the just exempt from any pain, from any disquietude, from the deformity that might blight its beauty, from the weakness that might destroy its health? Do you trust in God? Job, too, was close to the Lord. Are your friends and children your security? There is no hiding place in the world where trouble may not find you. No one knows when sorrow might visit his house any more than Job did.

As always, the visuals that accompany the sermon are crucial. As the pastor asks, "Is there some fraud in the scheme of the universe?" the camera focuses on R. L., whose death raises precisely this question for the O'Brien family. When Father Haynes asks, "Is there nothing that is deathless, nothing which does not pass away?" the camera pans up a stained glass window depicting Jesus on trial. Jesus is a Job-like innocent sufferer, but the scene and the sermon hint at the Christian conviction that the innocent suffering of Jesus is not just another instance of the disjointedness of the universe but

---

4. At this point, the scene cuts from the church service to Mr. O'Brien praying and lighting a candle, presumably for a dead church member.

somehow its solution. Somehow, this one innocent sufferer is the antidote to innocent suffering.

The thrust of the sermon is the hopeful message that one encounters God as much when God turns his back as when he turns his countenance.

> The very moment everything was taken away from Job he knew it was the Lord who'd taken it away. He turned from the passing shows of time. He sought that which is eternal.[5] Does he alone see God's hand who sees that he gives? Or does not also the one see God's hand who sees that he takes away? Or does he alone see God who sees God turn his face towards him? Does not also he see God who sees God turn his back?

This resolution is pure Kierkegaard. In one of his *18 Upbuilding Discourses*, Kierkegaard reflects on Job's response to his loss: "The Lord gave, the Lord took away; blessed be the name of the Lord." Job can bless God's name in the midst of excruciating suffering because he trusts that God is love. If God is love, then he is love in the midst of death and suffering as much as in the midst of joyous life. Faith that God is love is not based on the evidence of sight anyway. It's a *choice*, and having made the choice Job adopts a "hermeneutic of love" that interprets everything, including loss and death, in the light of divine love, interprets everything as gift. Malick's preacher quotes one passage in particular:

> Job traces everything back to God; he did not detain his soul and quench his spirit with deliberation or explanations that only feed and foster doubt, even though the person suspended in them does not even notice that. The very moment everything was taken from him, he knew that it was the Lord who had taken it away, and therefore in his loss he remained on good terms with the Lord, in his loss maintained intimacy with the Lord; he saw the Lord and therefore he did not see despair. Or does he alone see God's hand who sees that he gives, or does not also the one see God's hand who sees that he takes away? Or does he alone see God who sees God turn his face toward him, or does not also he see God who sees him turn his back,

---

5. Again, visuals are important, and create some ironic juxtapositions to the message of the sermon. As the pastor speaks of turning from "the passions shows of time," we see Jack leaping from pew to pew in an empty church, dancing before the Lord. As the pastor notes that Job "sought that which is eternal," Mr. O'Brien shakes hands with the men of the church, and gets into the car announcing that the man he just greeted "is a friend of mine" who "owns half the real estate in town." Mr. O'Brien has not yet begun to turn from passing shows to the eternal.

just as Moses continually saw nothing but the Lord's back? But the one who sees God has overcome the world.[6]

Kierkegaard and Malick agree: There is a vision of God available only to those who watch him depart.

Dostoevsky too is in the background.[7] *Brothers Karamazov* is also infused with Joban themes. Ivan's protest against God's world is that innocents suffer unavenged, and in support he presents a gruesome catalog of stunning cruelties. Ivan wants to turn in his ticket; he refuses to be party to a world scheme where happiness comes to some at the price of innocent tears. Dostoevsky did not believe that there was any philosophical answer to Ivan's objections. One cannot present an *argument* that solves the problem of evil. *Brothers Karamazov* offers a "non-Euclidean" response to Ivan. Instead of refuting his brother, Alyosha kisses him, and later Alyosha falls to the ground, embraces the earth, and waters it with his tears. Dostoevsky does not emphasize the centrality of faith in the way that the radical Protestant Kierkegaard does. For him, active *love*, compassion, forgiveness and kindness, not argument, is the only "answer" to a broken world, to humans that have wandered from or been expelled from Eden and its tree of life. Not *credo ut intelligam*; rather, *amo etsi non intelligo*. Not "I believe in order to understand" but "I love though I do not understand." Dostoevsky brings Job into the picture through the elder, Father Zossima. Zossima's life is one of active love, and his teaching encourages Alyosha to follow the same path. In one section of the novel, Zossima offers his reflections on the story of Job. How, he asks, could Job love the children that he received to replace the lost children?

---

6. Kierkegaard, *18 Upbuilding Discourses* (trans. Howard V. Hong and Edna H. Hong; Princeton: Princeton University Press, 1990), 121.

7. In a 2003 interview, Martin Sheen describes how Malick's gift of *The Brothers Karamzov* helped him return to his Catholic roots: "I went to Paris and ran into Terry, who'd been living there for a couple of years, and we got reacquainted and got very close, and he became a mentor in a lot of ways for me. He was able to see where I needed to focus and was able to guide me to a little clearer place. He would give me material, books to read. Finally, the last book he gave me was *The Brothers Karamazov*, and that book had a very profound effect on my spiritual life, and that was like the final door that I had to go through. I finished reading that, and it was May Day, and I went into what turned out to be the only English-speaking Catholic church in all of France. I had not gone to church in years. I came across an Irish priest. I told him I'd stayed away from the faith for a long time, and I'd like to make a confession. He said you come to see me Saturday afternoon at the appointed hour, and I did. That was for me the journey home. Terrence was key to my awakening." ("The Progressive Interview," http://martinsheen.net/id151.html.)

Job, praising the Lord, serves not only Him but all His creation for generations and generations, and for ever and ever, since for that he was ordained. Good heavens, what a book it is, and what lessons there are in it! What a book the Bible is, what a miracle, what strength is given with it to man! It is like a mold cast of the world and man and human nature, everything is there, and a law for everything for all the ages. And what mysteries are solved and revealed! God raises Job again, gives him wealth again. Many years pass by, and he has other children and loves them. But how could he love those new ones when those first children are no more, when he has lost them? Remembering them, how could he be fully happy with those new ones, however dear the new ones might be? But he could, he could.[8]

There is no answer, no argument. No rational proof could explain why Job loved his children after all he suffered. What stands is the simple fact of love: "He could, he could."

Like the great literary treatments of Job, *The Tree of Life* cannot avoid treating the whole history of the cosmos. Human suffering is not a local but a global and even cosmic matter. Malick knows that even the least tear of the most insignificant human being raises questions about the kind of universe we live in and the character of the power who made and runs it. Malick is enough a student of Kierkegaard and Dostoevsky to know that there is no straightforward rational argument that will explain evil. *The Tree of Life* is a non-Euclidian response to suffering which, like Job, involves the whole of history from creation to the end of time.

"Where were you?" Mrs. O'Brien asks as she mourns R. L.'s death. That is the question that leads into the eighteen-minute evolution sequence in the film. To Mrs. O'Brien's "Where were you?" the film returns to the opening quotation from Job where the Lord offers a "Where were you?" of his own: "Where were you when I laid the foundations of the earth, and the morning stars sang together?" A God who made such a world, a world designed for man, a world through which glory shines, should be loved and trusted. What is he doing? Where was he when R. L. died? He will not say. He says only as he said to Job, "I am love. Trust me, and love. Love every tree, every leaf, every drop of rain. Fall to the earth and embrace it. Love the world in all its ruin."

<hr>

8. *The Brothers Karamazov* (New York: Macmillan, 1922), 308.

Chapter 3

Water

"You let a boy drown. You'll do anything."

—Jack O'Brien

WATER HAS MANY DIFFERENT meanings in religion and literature. In the Bible, the world is first a liquid chaos until the ordered cosmos is born from the watery womb. Creation is hydraulics, as God moves waters above the firmament and then splits the waters on earth to reveal the dry land. Water is life. Water cleanses away impurities so that sinners can come into God's presence. Water kills. Noah's flood covers the earth with water again, marking the end of one creation and leading to the beginning of another, and the waters of the Red Sea that had opened to let Israel out close again to drown Pharaoh and his chariots. Rivers form boundaries, so that a water-crossing becomes an image of entry into a new life or a new status. Christian baptism embodies all these meanings and more: It is death to Adam and the flesh, new birth in the Spirit, cleansing and crossing, a new flood and a new exodus.

The first sound we hear in *The Tree of Life* is the sound of water. Ocean waves roll gently onto a beach, and we hear the gulls crying. We see none of it. Water is first heard, seen only later. First it beckons, and to see it we have to follow its beckoning. At the end of the film, the beach is the world reborn and rebaptized and all things are well. Before we know that there is any such promise of final reconciliation, its sound fills the air.

We first *see* water at the end of Mrs. O'Brien's opening discourse about nature and grace. She says, "The nuns told us that no one who walks in the way of grace comes to a bad end," as the camera moves toward R. L. then cuts to a waterfall. We see crashing water from above, and the camera moves down into the abyss below. It's a flood, a surging, powerful, deadly cascade that might sweep the world itself before it. "Terrors take him away like a flood" (Job 27:20). The threatening waters of death pose no threat in Jack's infancy. Jack plays with his mother in the yard, a wooden Noah's ark their favorite toy. During Jack's childhood, he is safe from the flood.[1] But water becomes a literal cause of death when a boy drowns in the swimming pool, and Jack feels as if he has been cast out of the safety of the ark into a watery world that might overwhelm him. He comes to "deep waters, and a flood overwhelms me" (Ps 69:2). The randomness of water leads Jack to accuse God of negligence, questioning God as his mother did when R. L. died: "Where were you? You let a boy drown. You'll do anything."

In Jack's memory, the water of childhood is mostly life-giving. He is born by swimming out of an underwater bedroom, and he is born into a boyhood that is moist, verdant, well-watered like a garden. Early in the film, when Jack remembers R. L. as a brave, kind, and good boy, he remembers him wet, hair drenched and wet shirt clinging to his chest. The boys are themselves trees of life, as Mr. O'Brien is shown in one scene spraying his shrieking boys with the garden hose. As Jack comes to realize how far he has drifted from his brother and from God, he asks "How do I get back to where they are?" while he swims with his brothers under a waterfall. It is like a second baptism. Boyhood is a baptism, a bubblebath, a river, a day of rain; it's swimming in rivers, pools, under a waterfall. The sound of water that opens the film beckons Jack back to the moistness of childhood. To be reconciled to the world, Jack has to be reconciled with the water world of his past. He will be born again by being rejoined with his wet younger self.

Rejoined too to the moistness of the childhood of the universe. Combining biblical and evolutionary imagery, Malick shows that water is the means for the birth of life as such. The creation/evolution sequence moves through shots of deep space to volcanic gurgling and explosions and eventually toward water. In the water grasses grow, the first vegetation, the beginnings of a tree of life. Spirals of what look like DNA corkscrew along, then jellyfish and tadpoles and other fish. Land animals eventually crawl out of the water, but even the land animals are always around water. In the last scene of the evolution sequence, we watch a meteor hit the oceans,

1. Several mysterious scenes in the film show the interior of the O'Brien's wood-floored, wood-paneled attic. With its curved walls, it looks like an inverted boat, the interior of an ark. It is a place of safety, of childhood innocence, where he rocks in a toddler rocking chair and rides his tricycle. But the place of safety remains with the adult Jack only in dreams.

sending shock waves across the globe. The world as we know it emerges after that flood subsides.

Malick also employs the traditional association of time with rivers. He fills in the period between Jack's toddlerhood and his teenage years with a sequence that begins with a river scene. We see a series of vignettes from Jack's early life—visits from grandparents, holding a goldfish, puzzling over the presence of a new child in the house. In the background, we hear Smetena's *Moldau*, an orchestral poem about a Czech river. Time passes like a river; the river flows toward the ocean of eternity. To reach the ocean, Jack has to follow the river of his life all the way to a vision of its end.

The Bible begins in a garden, a well-watered place. A river flows through, the garden is full of rich vegetation, and the tree of life stands in the middle of the garden. After Adam sins, he and Eve are expelled from the garden and humanity begins its sojourn in the wilderness. Israel wanders through the wilderness for forty years before entering the land, Elijah is driven into the wilderness to be fed by ravens, John begins his ministry in the wilderness, and Jesus goes to the wilderness to be tempted by the devil. In scripture, the desert is a place of testing, trial, temptation. It is the place of exile, where people long for the water and fruit of the garden. "O God, you are my God. Earnestly I seek for you. My soul thirsts for you, my flesh yearns for you, in a dry and weary land where there is no water" (Ps 63:1).

As time passes in the film, the river disappears and we find ourselves again and again with Jack in the wilderness. While Jack is at work on the anniversary of his brother's death, his mind alternates between past scenes of rivers and pools and scenes of present desolation. There is a rough wooden door in a blue and green doorway. The paint has faded and begun to chip. The door stands slightly open, letting a sliver of light into the interior. The walls look plastered or stucco, painted blue, stained here and there. Then a cut to the adult Jack before a free-standing doorway. It's the first time we see the adult Jack. He wears a business suit. Gulls circle and scream overhead, but he is not at the seashore. We don't know it yet from the first brief glimpse, but he is stumbling through a wilderness, desolate and dry, the terrain rough. He finds a shallow puddle of water and washes his face, then stares at his distorted reflection in the water. He runs up a dune, but there's only more desert on the other side. It's nothing but desert as far as he can see. The desert is an externalization of his soul, which is dry as a weary land. Instead of swimming along a river of life, Jack lives in a dry stream bed.

In the Christian tradition, the desert was the literal location for the earliest Christian ascetics. The Egyptian "desert fathers" escaped from both the decadence of late Roman culture and the growing compromises of the church to pursue God undistracted in the desert. Malick picks up again on the mystic tradition that speaks both of the "dark night of the soul" and of the "desert of the soul." Thomas a Kempis prays in *The Imitation of Christ*,

> O Lord my God, You are all my good. And who am I that I should dare to speak to You? I am Your poorest and meanest servant, a vile worm, much more poor and contemptible than I know or dare to say. Yet remember me, Lord, because I am nothing, I have nothing, and I can do nothing. You alone are good, just, and holy. You can do all things, You give all things, You fill all things: only the sinner do You leave empty-handed. Remember Your tender mercies and fill my heart with Your grace, You Who will not allow Your works to be in vain. How can I bear this life of misery unless You comfort me with Your mercy and grace? Do not turn Your face from me. Do not delay Your visitation. Do not withdraw Your consolation, lest in Your sight my soul become as desert land. Teach me, Lord, to do Your will. Teach me to live worthily and humbly in Your sight, for You are my wisdom Who know me truly, and Who knew me even before the world was made and before I was born into it.[2]

After Jack rises from bed early on the morning of the anniversary of his brother's death, he goes to the bathroom and turns on the faucet. A stream of clear water flows from the shiny steel pipe, and Jack plays with the flow with his fingers, remembering the moistness of his boyhood. He needs water, longs for water, not only for refreshment but for cleansing. Grief is not the only weight he bears; he bears also a burden of guilt. Is there enough water in all the world to wash it all away? Will the ocean that beckons be a fountain for cleansing as well as a return to innocent childhood?

Jack is not the only one with a desert in his soul. He inherited the desert from his father. As Mr. O'Brien walks down the street and talks to Jack about his failed dreams, about how life passed him by, there is a momentary shot of a desolate wasteland, whipped by wind-blown sand. Mr. O'Brien failed early, almost accidentally. He dreamed of being a great musician, and he had talent. Music was not just a career dream, but an obsession. He can hardly listen to the conversation of his wife and children at the dinner table when Brahms starts playing. He stands in front of his record

---

2. Thomas, *The Imitation of Christ*, 3, available at http://www.ccel.org/ccel/kempis/ imitation.THREE.3.html.

player conducting the music. He takes his cues about hard work, perfection, and achievement from Toscanini. But he abandoned the dream as "life got in the way." Before he knew it, he was stuck. During Jack's boyhood, Mr. O'Brien works in a generic factory,[3] and in that setting he can fancy himself a big man. He strides around through warehouses and around huge machines and across the catwalks, pointing to his watch and giving directions. Already then his soul is shriveled. Toward the end of the film his career comes crashing down. The plant closes, and he is offered only a job that no one wants. Now he has failed at two careers, the one he never started and the one he devoted the best years of his life to.

To cover his failures, Mr. O'Brien invents success stories. Mr. O'Brien pages through a notebook full of drawings of his inventions, and he boasts to his boys of many patents. Courtroom scenes tell a different story. We see only the end of the court cases, Mr. O'Brien sitting at the table, his posture a mixture of resignation and rage, as one of his attorneys says "we'll get them next time." He goes on a worldwide sales trip, but comes back with little more than promises of future ventures. Sometimes his tall tales are pathetically funny. He flew around the world on Pan Am Airlines, whose planes are equipped with stainless steel bathrooms. Everything is stainless steel, he says, "even the sink." (Perhaps this was impressive in the 1950s.) He shows off the Chinese characters on the towels he brings back from the trip, and we cannot help but wonder if he stole the towels from a hotel. Mr. O'Brien's soul is shrunken with shame, and he passes his own sense of failure and shame to his boys.

Out of his failures, Mr. O'Brien emerges as a hardened, cynical man. Despite his own inability to control his destiny, he assures his sons that they can: "You make yourself what you are. You have control of your own destiny. Never say 'I can't.' Say, 'I'm having trouble. I'm not done yet.'" He teaches his sons to play loose with moral concerns. "You can't be too good," he advises his sons, criticizing his "naïve" wife who thinks that you can just love your way through life. You have to play rough if you want to get ahead: "You gotta sew them up. Get em by the nuts." He trains his boys with a regiment of masculine toughness, but since it emerges from his own weakness and failure, all he teaches them is the way of the desert, where there is no tree of life.

As an adult, Jack is far more successful than his father. He lives in a clean upscale house of windows, and he works at the top of a glass

---

3. Mr. O'Brien always calls it "the plant," as though he thinks of it as a garden or tree. In "the plant," there is nothing organic anywhere to be seen. It's all metal and concrete.

skyscraper, where he seems to hold a high position in an architectural firm. He has achieved the success his father always longed for. But Jack's demeanor throughout the film indicates success in this form is hollow, stale, tasteless. Life passes by the successful and the failures, unless they see the glory that smiles through everything. From this perspective, Jack is a modern Everyman. He has pursued career, success, and money, and it's all worked. He is at the top of the world, regularly ascending in an elevator to offices high above the city. Inside, he is dead. Nothing grows. "O God, you are my God. Earnestly I seek for you. My soul thirsts for you, my flesh yearns for you, in a dry and weary land where there is no water" (Ps 63:1).[4]

Yet there are those waves, the sound of water in the desert, the gulls crying above like the sons of God who greeted the first dawn of creation. Jack is in the desert, but there is a doorway in the desert, and perhaps that door leads to the oceanside. But Jack cannot get from the desert to the ocean on his own. He needs a guide from the wilderness to the sea, and the film gives several pillars of cloud and fire that will guide him. The credits of *Tree of Life* list a character named only "Guide," played by Jessica Fuselier. She has no lines, and we rarely see her face. Her back is toward the camera in most of her scenes, and in some we see only her body, her hands. She is a mysterious, half-seen presence, who "guides them in the wilderness like a flock" (Ps 78:52).

Mysterious and half-seen, but always present.[5] The Guide first brought Jack into the world. Toward the middle of the film, we see Mr. O'Brien stroking the pregnant belly of his wife, leaning down to listen, awestruck, to the heartbeat of his unborn son. The camera cuts to an iron gate, opening into a grove or a garden, while a hand points someone to walk through. A woman in white with her back to the camera, and holding a candle, leans down to whisper in the ear of a small boy, Jack, who stands beside a stream. The camera ascends a set of old steps, grass growing through the cracks in

---

4. There is perhaps a hint of Eliot here: "The dead tree gives no shelter, the cricket no relief, / And the dry stone no sound of water. . . . I will show you something different from either / Your shadow at morning striding behind you / Or your shadow at evening rising to meet you; / I will show you fear in a handful of dust" ("The Wasteland," lines 23–30). Malick's concern with the problem of healing time might owe something to Eliot's *Four Quartets*.

5. In one scene, she veils R. L.'s face with the window curtain and kisses him, and we glimpse her standing outside the screen door of the O'Brien house. After the funeral of the drowned boy, a woman gives Jack a sip of water from a clay cup, and washes him. Perhaps this is Mrs. O'Brien, but the hands seem to be the hands of the Guide, cleansing and refreshing him, renewing his baptismal faith, shattered by the watery death of his friend.

the stone, and shows us a monstrous grimacing face of stone. It's the "Door to Hell," one of the sculptures in Pier Francesco Orsini's Renaissance-era Garden of Monsters in Bomarzo, Italy. In the verdant, lush surroundings, the image arrests and jolts us:

> Paradise, Earth, and Hell are then all commingling in Malick's world. To enter Life is to enter Hell, and yet the moment is filmed and felt with such lushness and tranquility that we feel like we are being birthed into an earthly paradise. The Door to Hell is a Hell-Mouth, an archetype in Christian mythology which also, interestingly, corresponds to the Leviathan from Job (the Leviathan's jaws are often referred to as the jaws of Hell), then tying this image up all the more with the paradoxical image of the Plesiosaur and the dual nature of God.[6]

This is overstated, and suggests that Malick is more of a dualist and a Gnostic than the film allows. Yet it is true that for Malick, birth is entry into a world that has its hells. Every child enters the world of Job, where bad things happen to good people.

Yet Jack passes through the door to hell with a guide. The woman appears again, extending a hand of help and welcome, beckoning a few children who walk carefully over the rocks toward the river that they will soon cross. She shows the Jack a tiny book, and then guides a line of children through the forest, laying her hand gently on the back of Jack's head. Then we are in an underwater womb-room, watching Jack swim out the birth canal toward a light. A woman swims upward ahead of him, a bridal veil streaming from her head behind her. It is the Guide, who has guided Jack into the world. The Guide leads through the doorway of the womb into the world.

When the Guide appears with the adult Jack in the wilderness, she is not an agent of birth but an agent of rebirth. The contrast of the two scenes is stark. Initially, she is in a room full of water, or at the banks of a river. She swims ahead of Jack toward the light of the world. In his adulthood, Jack's life has been dried out, and the Guide leads him through the wilderness of his soul. She is the cloud that leads Jack through the wilderness toward the promised land.

The symbolism of the doorway in the desert is too obvious, but it is important to catch the subtlety of the image. To all appearances, the doorway leads *nowhere*. There's nothing but desert on the other side. Even after

---

6. "Terrence Malick's Song of Himself," http://nilesfilmfiles.blogspot.com/2011/06/song-of-himself-terrence-malicks-tree.html.

Jack passes through it, he is still in the desert. His hesitations at the doorway indicate that he knows that the doorway is significant, but passing through requires an act of faith. He cannot see anything better ahead. He can only see the Guide who brought him into this world, beckoning him forward. What does she know? She led him through the door of hell! But against all appearances, he takes a leap of faith and steps through.

Immediately, two things happen. The camera rushes toward the Guide's abdomen, her dress floating in the breeze. The moment recalls Mr. O'Brien's raptured listening at the pregnant belly of his wife. The Guide births a new Jack, and immediately Malick cuts to an image from the creation: A small dark dot of a planet moves past a tangle of red and yellow clouds and flame. Creation is happening all over again. It is a new creation. Stepping through the doorway is a new birth. Though it looked as if there was nothing but desert on the other side, in fact it is a new creation, a chapel with a ladder that reaches toward heaven, an ocean. By stepping through the doorway toward a new life, Jack is participating in a cosmic rebirth. "Keep us, guide us," Jack whispers, and he is not only talking about himself or his family. It is a prayer for divine guidance that will take the universe to the end of time, which repeats the first dawn of creation.

The second thing that happens is that the Guide disappears. She reappears a few minutes later, dressed as a bride, beckoning and leading toward the beach. But her guidance of Jack basically ends. She has taken Jack to the doorway, shown him the way through, but the last part of the journey she leaves to another. Adult Jack's guide in the last part of his desert trek is his younger self. Young Jack races up a small rock, climbs through an opening in a wall of rock, and the camera leads us up a dock on a beach. Following his younger self, Jack finds his way to the beach. Once he recovers his younger self, Jack can find his way out of the labyrinth, out of the deserted isolation of his life. Reunited with his own past self, he can come to the ocean's edge where he can be reunited with R. L. and everyone else.

When Jack finally reaches the beach, the Guide walks *behind* him, and as he kneels on the wet sand she strikes the back of his head, repeating the gesture of his journey from the womb into the world. Kneeling on the beach, Jack folds his hands over her feet and does homage to the Guide who has led him to the end of his journey. The Guide that brought him from the watery womb returns him to the font at which he was first committed "manfully" to fight the assaults of the world, the flesh, and the devil. Jack finds the water of youth. He discovers an ocean that will cleanse his guilt.

Chapter 4

Flame

"My hope. My God."

—Mrs. O'Brien

THE FIRST VISUAL IN *The Tree of Life* is a faint orange flame. Like a curtain in a breeze, it quietly emerges, complicates, folds, grows, intensifies, folds again and again, then fades out. The film ends with the sounds of waves and gulls and we see the flame again, now multicolored, blues and greens folding in and out of oranges and yellows. Already in the first shot, we have a glimpse of the end. In the Alpha flame, we already anticipate the Omega. In between, the flame appears twice against a black background. After the opening sequence that shows the O'Briens' response to R. L.'s death, it reappears, marking a transition in time, as the camera races forward in a smear of color from R. L.'s death to the "present" of Jack's adulthood. The flame appears at the beginning of the evolution sequence. It thus marks the temporal seams of the film, dividing it into three main sections:

1. R.L.'s death.
2. Jack's adulthood.
3. Creation and evolution.

What is intriguing about this structure is that the flame does *not* separate the creation/evolution sequence from the story of the O'Brien family. Creation and evolution do not form a separate story from that of the O'Briens. The O'Brien saga, small and common as it is, is the climax of the massive work of creation. All creation provides the setting in which this small family drama unfolds. Human beings with all their frailties and foibles are the topmost branches on the evolutionary tree of life.

The first three times the flame appears, a voice prays in voice-over. Jack whispers "Brother. Mother" in the first scene, and his voice whispers "How did you come to me?" at the flame's second appearance. The third time, Mrs. O'Brien asks, "Lord, why? Where were you?" Only at the end are there no voices, but instead the sound of waves and gulls, then birds and crickets, as the flame fades and the credits begin to roll. When all is done, prayer yields to silence, and creation sings, as it did on when the Lord laid the foundation of the world and the morning stars sang together.

Fire is a commonplace religious image. To Israel in the wilderness, Yahweh appears in a cloud that glowed with fire during the night, and this gleaming glory descends from Sinai into the most holy place of the tabernacle. On the altar is a smaller fire into which sacrifices were placed and turned to smoke as they ascended to God. The book of Hebrews uses these images when it declares that "our God is a consuming fire" (Heb 12:29). When Jesus was transfigured, his robe became as bright as light; the Spirit marks the apostles in the upper room with dancing flames on their heads; in Revelation Jesus's eyes are like flames of fire. Ancient Romans thought that the flame on the home hearth represented the fiery spirit of the ancestors who were still with them, still sharing their meals. Zororastrians do not, as often charged, worship fire, but they consider fire a symbol of spiritual purification, and in Vedic Hinduism, fire is a mediator between the worshiper and the gods.

God is fire; humans are images of God; therefore, for many religions, the human soul is a divine spark, a small flicker from the eternal flame of the deity. Malick plays off of this symbolism early in the film. As Jack gets ready for work, he stands in the kitchen flicking a lighter into a blue candle cylinder on the counter. He watches the light as he wife looks over his shoulder. Jack says, "My brother died when he was nineteen," and the screen goes black. R. L. was a light radiant with the light of grace, but his flame went out prematurely. Later, Mr. O'Brien lights a candle after church, perhaps in memory of someone who has died, and in the procession of resurrection at the end of the film children carry candles.

Creation as a whole emerges from fire. The evolution sequence begins with the divine fire, which fades to black. Then streaks of white smoke float from the left of the screen, some of them moving in the slow dance of the divine flame, some of them refracting light to make a rainbow. Galaxies, nebulae and planets are first a red cloud in the middle of the screen, and then a bright white light shines passes through dark red clouds—all variations on the divine light that called the worlds into being. Earth itself is a ball hung on nothing, ringed by the sun, and as we get closer we see it is a molten planet, surging and crashing as meteors pelt it from miles above. All creation partakes of the flame. Creation mirrors the divine glory back to the Creator.

Though the divine flame does not mark the beginning of the O'Brien family story, faint images of the divine light appear again and again in the second half of the film. "When did you first touch my heart?" Jack asks, and there is a cut to a street light shining against a dark background of branches and leaves. The light was there even before Jack was, certainly before he was aware of the light. Mr. and Mrs. O'Brien embrace in a room, possibly on their wedding night, as car lights flash like a strobe through the windows, illuminating them in various poses. As infant Jack lies in a crib sucking his thumb, his mother sings and a white light dances on the green wall of the bedroom. In the next shot, the moon shines above the O'Brien house through a blur of nighttime clouds, again resembling the divine light. Light jumps on the wall in a stairwell. The light is there later when the boys come running to the house for dinner, captured now in the house light that stands guard at the O'Brien's doorway. After tucking the boys into bed, Mr. O'Brien leaves the door open so a light can shine through, and the camera moves in tight on the night light plugged into the wall socket. Malick cuts from the night light to a scene in the "upper room," the wood-paneled ark-attic with a bright window at one end. It is at the top of the staircase, just as God lives (Mrs. O'Brien tells infant R. L.) up in the heavens, where the sun shines. At the end of the film, as the O'Briens drive away from their home, the camera turns to the sky, where a pink sun gilds a few surrounding clouds. The flame goes with them, leading them through the wilderness toward the return to the garden, back to the tree of life. The flame is the Alpha and Omega of the movie, and reminders of that flame stand at the the beginning and end of the main plot, the story of the O'Briens' early life in Waco.

Jack wanders, he tells us. In one of the most pronounced Augustinian touches in a very Augustinian film, the light tells a different story. "Late have I loved you, O Beauty ever ancient, ever new," Augustine says in one of the most famous passages of the *Confessions*. "Late have I loved you. You were within me, but I was outside, and it was there that I searched for you. In my unloveliness I plunged into the lovely things which you created. You were with me, but I was not with you."[1] No matter how far Jack wanders, no matter how much he ignores the light, the light watches over him, drawing him back. He has never been far from the light, just as he has never been without a Guide.

It is also thoroughly Augustinian for Malick to emphasize that the divine flame is mediated through human flames. As the fire flickers on the screen in the opening shot, we hear the first words of the film, the adult Jack whispering in a voice-over, "Mother. Brother." It has the hushed quality of prayer, and soon it does resolve into explicit prayer: "It was they who led me to your door." The first two words are the film's main answer to Jack's question, "How did you come to me? In what shape? What disguise?" Jack doesn't idolize his mother and brother but recognizes them as mediators of the divine presence, as guides that brought him to the door of the place where God lives, as channels of the grace that Jack received before he knew who was giving it.[2] Augustine similarly writes of the gifts that "sustained me from the first moment," even before the time he can remember. From his mother's breast, Augustine says, he received the first gifts of divine grace: "It was by Your gift that I desired what You gave and no more, by Your gift that those who suckled me willed to give me what You had given them: for it was by the love implanted in them by You that they gave so willingly that milk which by Your gift flowed in the breasts."[3] For Jack, Mrs. O'Brien is the feminine form of the divine presence, and God's presence is mediated to Mrs. O'Brien in turn by her children, especially by her beloved R. L. "My son, my soul," she says as she grieves for him. He is her hope, her future, her life, not because he is her God but because she came to know hope and to experience life through his presence. Losing him, she fears she has lost the God who gave him.

I have never seen a film so drenched in prayer as *The Tree of Life*. During the film's first half hour, there is more prayer than dialogue. Most of the

1. Augustine, *Confessions*, trans. Albert Outler (Mineola, NY: Dover Thrift Editions), 10.27.

2. In the scene where Jack first encounters baby R. L., we momentarily hear waves on the beach. Before Jack is in the desert looking for water, we know that R. L. will be the one to call him there. R. L. and Mrs. O'Brien were mediators, but not the only ones, as Jack recognizes in a voice-over just after the creation sequence ends: "You spoke to me through her. You spoke with me from the sky. The trees. Before I knew I loved you, believed in you."

3. Augustine, *Confessions*, trans. Albert Outler (Mineola, NY: Dover Thrift Editions), I, 3–14.

prayers occur in voice-overs. In a number of scenes, we do witness public prayer. Mr. O'Brien is a praying man. He opens dinner with prayer, and we see him alone in a room kneeling in earnest prayer after R. L.'s death. He prays in church after everyone else but Jack has left the building. But we never hear Mr. O'Brien's inner prayers. His prayers are external, formal, repetitive.[4] The contrast between the two forms of prayer is most evident in a scene where twelve-year-old Jack kneels at his bed praying. Out loud, he prays a typical adolescent prayer about help with typical adolescent challenges: "Help me not to sass my dad. Help me not to get dogs in fights. Help me be thankful for everything I got. Help me not to tell lies." In voice-overs that begin even while his formal prayers continue, young Jack expresses his longing to know God: "Where do you live? Are you watching me? I want to know what you are. I want to see what you see." As Jack admits later in the film, he is a unstable combination of his two parents: "Mother, father, always you wrestle inside me, always you will." The wrestling is not least of all a wrestling about the way of prayer.

The voice-overs are the secret prayers of the heart. Surrounded by women mourning R. L.'s death with her, Mrs. O'Brien laments, "My hope, my God," then, in a wonderful depiction of the mercurial modulations of the soul, her voice interrupts her own voice-over with a quotation from Psalm 23, "I will fear no evil."[5] She whispers again, "What did you gain," and then interrupts herself with Psalm 22:11 "Be not far from me, for trouble is near." Psalm 23 is famously a psalm of comfort from the Lord who is the "shepherd" of his people. The second Psalm begins with "My God, My God! Why have you forsaken me?"—the cry of dereliction that Jesus utters on the cross. Mrs. O'Brien is stretched between the two psalms, between the hope for comfort and the pain of loss.

In the Joban setting of *Tree of Life*, it's unsurprising that the prayers often express grief and lamentation. Nor are all of these lamentations articulated in words. Mrs. O'Brien's initial response to the news of R. L.'s

---

4. For that matter, we only hear the inner prayers of Jack and Mrs. O'Brien. Not even R. L. prays in a voice-over. That is in part, surely, because the film belongs to Jack. It's his story of loss and recovery, of wandering and return, and his mother's influence is crucial in that. Yet the difference between the prayers of Mr. and Mrs. O'Brien reinforce the contrast of two ways of coming to God's door.

5. Though somewhat clumsy, Malick's voice-overs frequently give texture and depth to a scene. We see Mrs. O'Brien with her friends, but her mind is occupied with something else, with several thoughts at once, in fact. This lends a psychological complexity and realism to the film, as well as an emotional depth.

death is to cry out "O God," a cry that is cut off before she gets it out. In the following minutes of the film, we hear disembodied shrieks and cries. The Spirit groans with sorrows too deep for words. Many of the prayers are, like Job's and Augustine's, in the interrogative mood. The O'Briens do not ask for things, not even for comfort in sorrow. They pose their puzzlement to God. They don't want help from God. They want answers, answers to their sense of the disarray of the universe. While a cloud of birds swirls over a city, we hear Mrs. O'Brien's Joban prayer, "Why? Where were you? Did you know? Who are we to you? Answer me!" Those birds contain the beginning of an answer, an answer that is related to the divine flame that opens the film. That flame of glory shines through all things, including the undulating cloud of birds. To questions like Mrs. O'Brien's, the film gives the same answer that comes to Job: There is no answer but God himself, the flame at the heart of all things, the flame that bursts out in a world aflame with the glory of God. It is an answer, the non-Euclidian answer that is the only answer there is. At the beginning of the creation sequence, Mrs. O'Brien asks, "Why? Where were you?" She falls silent as we watch the worlds take form, and when she comes back she is no longer questioning but calling on God to hear: "We cry to you. My soul. My son. Hear us." The creation sequence ends with Mrs. O'Brien praying in hope, "Light of my life. I search for you. My hope. My child."

Adult Jack's prayers turn into questioning laments: "How did I lose you?" But Jack's prayers and Mrs. O'Brien's turn to challenges. "Where were you?" Mrs. O'Brien asks. When a well-meaning friend assures her that R. L. is "in God's hands now," Mrs. O'Brien issues a whispered rebuke, "He was in God's hands all the time, wasn't he?" After Jack's friend drowns in the swimming pool, Jack demands an explanation from God: "Was he bad? You let a boy drown. You'll do anything." And the capriciousness of God draws the question, "Why should I be good, when you're not?"

Impious as these might sound, Malick has solid biblical precedent for such prayers. Job presents some of the most severe complaints against God that we find in all literature:

> Why did I not die at birth, come forth from the womb and expire? (Job 3:11).

> The arrows of the Almighty are within me; their poison my spirit drinks; the terrors of God are arrayed against me (Job 6:4).

Have I sinned? What have I done to Thee, O watcher of men? Why hast thou set me as Thy target, so that I am a burden to myself? (Job 7:20).

I desire to argue with God (Job 13:3).

Oh that I knew where I might find Him, that I might come to His seat! I would present my case before Him and fill my mouth with arguments (Job 23:3–4).

My soul is poured out within me; days of affliction have seized me. At night it pierces my bones within me, and my gnawing pains take no rest. By a great force my garment is distorted; it binds me about as the collar of my coat. He has cast me into the mire, and I have become like dust and ashes. I cry out to Thee for help, but thou does not answer me; I stand up, and Thou dost turn Thy attention against me. Thou has become cruel to me, with the might of Thy hand thou does persecute me (Job 30:16–21).

Like Job, Malick seems to know that God created human beings to talk back to him.

The film has no whirlwind scene, no voice from heaven setting everything right. The God to which Jack and Mrs. O'Brien pray remains a flame, always there, always shining through everything, but never simply there for the grabbing. He cannot be held or held down. He is elusive as fire that emerges, complicates, folds, grows, intensifies, folds again and again, then seems to fade out just when you need him most.

Chapter 5

Music

"I wanted to be a great musician."

—Mr. O'Brien

Music plays a prominent role in *The Tree of Life*. In addition to the "trance-like" and "meditative" minimalist score composed for the film by Alexandre Desplat,[1] Malick makes use of a wide variety of art music. The film opens with John Tavener's *Funeral Canticle*, the *Vlatava/Moldau* of Berdich Smetana plays through a long sequence, and a long sequence at the end is backed by the *Agnus Dei* of Berlioz's *Grande Messe des Morts* (or *Requiem*). Along the way there is music from Mahler, Respighi, Holst, Mussorgsky, and Gorecki.

In addition to the music that plays in the background of the action, music plays an important part in the plot. Mr. O'Brien once dreamed of being a concert pianist, and his life is tinged with the bitterness of having abandoned that dream. He interrupts his wife's dinner-table summary of the day to turn up a record playing Brahms's *Fourth Symphony*, which he pretends to direct. During one scene, he takes Jack to watch him play Bach's *Toccata and Fugue in D Minor* on a large pipe organ. R. L. plays

---

1. The descriptions are from Desplat himself (quoted in the Oscar press kit for *The Tree of Life*, available online at http://www.oscars.org/press/presskits/nominations/pdf/84/04-tree-of-life.pdf). He goes on to say that Malick asked for music that would flow "like a body of water throughout the film. So there was a river-like feeling to what I tried to achieve. The music had ot be very organic so we used only live instruments and no electronics. There is a lot of piano, which is very simple and basic. And even though the movie is very spiritual, I didn't want the music to ever be New Age-y. I wanted a timeless quality, a shimmering quality, where vibrations arise from the sounds of nature."

the guitar, as did Malick's brother Larry, who committed suicide in 1968. When Mr. and Mrs. O'Brien first hear the news of R. L.'s death, the camera pans through the house, passing the doorway of R. L.'s room. His guitar is prominently displayed on its stand.

In one touching and important scene, Mr. O'Brien sits at the piano playing Bach. R. L. is visible through the screen door, sitting on the front porch with his guitar. Mr. O'Brien realizes that R. L. is harmonizing with him, and for a few moments they play together. Music establishes communion between father and son. Then there is a cut to Jack, stalking angrily through the yard listening to the music. Despite his conflicts with his father, R. L. has been able to find a way to harmonize that Jack has never found. Jack stands outside the communion of music.

Listing the composers and music, and examining Mr. O'Brien's musical dreams, does not do justice to the way that Malick employs music, sometimes as symbol, sometimes to add emotional or intellectual inflection to a scene, sometimes as allusion to connect scenes to one another.

Funeral music fills the movie. Before we know that the movie is about a young man's death, the music prepares us for mourning. Tavener's *Funeral Canticle* opens the film, coloring the background as Mrs. O'Brien talks about the ways of nature and grace. During the opening section of the evolution sequence, we listen to the heartbreaking soprano solo of Zbigniew Preisner's *Lacrimosa*, part of the *Requiem for my friend* that he composed at the death of Polish filmmaker Krzysztof Kieslowski in 1996. A brief piano solo of *Lacrimosa* returns later in the film. Tavener's *Resurrection in Hades* comes in later.

To say that the film's music is funereal is not to say that it is ultimately bleak or depressing. *Lacrimosa* is a lament, but the Latin text anticipates resurrection and final judgment, and offer hope for peace: "*Huic ergo parce, Deus: Pie Jesu Domine, Dona eis requiem.* In mercy spare, O God; Pitying Lord Jesus, Give your eternal rest." Malick selects the *Agnus Dei*, part of the penultimate movement of Berlioz's *Requiem*. Again, the text is a plea for mercy from the Lamb *qui tollis peccata mundi* (who takes away the sins of the world), and resolves in a plea for peace (*dona nobis pacem*). Malick uses Tavener's *Funeral Canticle*, with its Greek text, drawn from the Greek Orthodox funeral service, that reflects on life's inevitable griefs, its shadowy mutability, and asks for peace for the soul "in the light of Thy countenance, O Christ, and in the sweetness of Thy beauty." The canticle is punctuated by hallelujahs, which Malick uses.

Malick has chosen *Christian* funeral music, and infuses lament with hope for eternal life and resurrection. If this world is, as much of the Christian tradition has it, a "vale of tears," it is one that finally leads to eternal light, toward the oceanside where all is forgiven, all is healed. The whole film is a requiem, as Jack passes through the questions, laments, and pleas that death inevitably provokes, toward a final resolution in peace. The music is funereal, but it reaches toward *resquiat in pacem*.

Malick juxtaposes music and visuals to give depth to many moments of the film. Sometimes, he uses music that aurally matches what we see. When Smetana's *Moldau* begins, we are looking at a river (the Colorado, standing in for the Brazos near Waco). Smetana's symphonic poem depicts the Vlatava river and musically recounts the history of the Czech Republic.[2] Even in the music, the river becomes a river of time, a river of history, and in the film the visuals change from the river scene to a rapid series of vignettes from the childhood of the O'Brien boys. *Moldau* tells us that the river is the O'Brien's river of time, and the next time the river shows up in the film it is playing the same role, even though *Moldau* is no longer playing in the background. The music creates a symbolic river to accompany the literal river.

Lacrimosa plays in the background at the beginning of the evolution sequence. A friend suggests that the music unmasks Malick as a Gnostic. Gnosticism confuses creation and fall. Evil is not an intrusion into a good work, but is inherent in the material of creation. For Gnostics, the limitations of created life—temporality, bodiliness, need—are not good gifts from a Creator, as they are in orthodox Christianity. Rather, these features are unfortunate restrictions on human freedom and spirituality, and the Gnostic's goal is to wriggle free of constraint to realize his true, immaterial nature. Gnostics would find *Lacrimosa* a suitable response to the evolution of life as we know it. *Sunt lacrimae rerum*; here are the tears of things. For Gnostics, evil is the most basic and final reality of the world, and lamentation and tears are the appropriate human response.

---

2. It is also the source of the Israeli National Anthem. When we hear the rolling woodwinds open the piece, Mrs. O'Brien is spinning around holding one of her infant boys. She points to the sky and says, "That's where God lives." As Anthony Lane has said, the moment puts some "Judeo" into the Christian vision of Malick's film. See Lane, Lane, "Time Trip," *The New Yorker*, May 30, 2011, available at www.newyorker.com /arts/critics/cinema/2011/05/30/110530crci_cinema_lane.

I don't think this is Malick's intention.[3] Just before the evolution sequence, Mrs. O'Brien asks God in an anguished voice-over, "Where were you?" The film answers by recounting the evolution of the universe and of life, an answer based, as we have seen, on the biblical book of Job. The tears of the *Lacrimosa* are Mrs. O'Brien's as she laments R. L.'s death, and the musical lament reminds us that creation is God's response of "Where were you?" to Mrs. O'Brien's, "Where were you?" As we watch stunning pictures of distant galaxies and special effects depicting the formation of the creation, *Lacrimosa* continues. It fills the universe, resounding all the way to its edges, all the way to the God who made it. The sequence doesn't suggest the Gnostic idea that creation is a grand mistake; it expresses the cosmic dimensions of human grief.

Music also unites distant scenes together. The Tavener piece that opens the film reappears briefly later, during the film's most intense family conflict. Its reintroduction in the aftermath of a family fight works at several levels: It hints at a tragedy darker than the family drama we are watching, reminding us that the film is about how R. L.'s death infuses all of life. But the same music has been associated early on with grace, and we are reminded of the wisdom of the nuns in the initial scene. Despite the conflict at the family table, those who live in the way of grace can still see love smiling through all things.

3. I address the charge of Gnosticism and dualism again in the next chapter.

Chapter 6

Nature and Grace, Father and Mother

"The nuns taught us that there are two ways through life, the way of nature and the way of grace."

—Mrs. O'Brien

The Tree of Life opens with a girl—a young Mrs. O'Brien—looking out of a barn window. A breeze plays gently with her hair and swings the shutters back and forth. In a voice-over, Mrs. O'Brien recounts the lessons about nature and grace she learned from the nuns at Catholic school.

Nature and grace play a variety of roles in philosophy and theology. "Nature" is synonymous in modern usage with the world of mountains and forests, oceans and rivers, the atmosphere and outer space, and all the creatures that inhabit these realms. Given that Mrs. O'Brien learned what she knows from nuns, the theological uses of the terms seem the most relevant.

In theology, "nature" is ambiguous. It can refer to the characteristics and properties of a thing as God created it. Birds fly because it is in their nature to do so. Men made in the image of God naturally pray. Christians believe that nature in this sense is wholly good, since it comes from a good Creator. For ancient Stoics, nature so understood imposed ethical obligations: Humans should live and behave in ways that are consistent with their nature as human beings. It is morally wrong to act out of accord with nature. Many Christian thinkers have adapted Stoic concepts of nature in Christian ethical systems.

Christianity, though, also claims that nature has been corrupted by sin. In many traditions, human beings are said to have a "sinful nature" inherited in some fashion from the first man, Adam, and reinforced by both bad example and bad habits. This nature doesn't incline human beings to act humanly but to act in ways contrary to their best nature as human beings. "Concupiscence," translated as "lust" or, more accurately, "evil desire," impels human beings to every evil thing. Envy, hatred, sexual passions, pride, gluttony are all expressions of this sinful "nature."

"Grace" has a different sense depending on which of these ideas of "nature" it's joined to. When linked with "nature" understood as the created goodness of creatures, "grace" is the unmotivated goodness of God that moves him to create. He doesn't create because he needs anything, but out of his gracious desire to bestow his goodness and glory. In some versions of Catholic theology, grace in relation to created nature took on a more technical meaning. According to some threads of Catholic thought, "nature" as originally created was unstable. Because it was made from nothing, it tended toward nothing, or, because it was material, it inclined human beings toward sensuality. A human being with physical eyes and physical hands is "naturally" tantalized by the things that he can see and touch, and thereby drawn away from God. To keep created nature stable, and to ensure that Adam wasn't drawn away from God, God "superadded" grace to created nature. This extra layer was "supernatural" grace. When Adam sinned, this *donum superadditum* was stripped off, leaving human beings to their unstable, sensually inclined "natural" selves. Human beings were, in short, created with two layers—nature and grace—but sin reduced them to a single layer, still good, but inclined toward evil or toward nothingness.[1]

"Grace" is also used in conjunction with "nature" in the second sense. Grace is God's answer to the fall of Adam. In this sense "grace" means that God gives good things to the *un*deserving. He is compassionate not merely toward those who have not earned his favor; he is compassionate even toward those who have sinned and earned his anger and judgment. Grace is God's motivation for saving mankind. Sinful human beings are delivered from their self-destructive sinfulness by the grace of God.

Mrs. O'Brien's nuns don't exactly teach any of this. According to them, "nature" and "grace" name two ways of life. Mrs. O'Brien talks about the

1. One of the most important developments in Catholic theology in the past century was a wholesale attack on this two-layer model of human beings. The French Jesuit Henri de Lubac and others claimed instead that nature was already graced, already a manifestation of God's goodness. De Lubac showed that Thomas Aquinas, thought to be a proponent of the two-layer view, was nothing of the kind. Thomas did not think that human beings needed a second, supernatural layer. Rather, Thomas taught that human beings have a *natural* inclination toward the supernatural. Simply because they are created by God and in his image, they desire to be united to him in the final beatific vision at the end of time.

way of grace first. Those who live by the way of grace do not try to please themselves. Grace "accepts being slighted, forgotten disliked. Accepts insults and injuries." The way of grace is the way of meekness and humility. It is also, we find, the way of wonder. Those who live by grace see that "love is smiling through all things."

The way of nature fights again being slighted. It seeks its own pleasure, and strives to "get others to please it too." One who lives by nature wants to "lord it over" others, "to have its own way." Because nature seeks its own way and wants to control and dominate, it does not accept, does not receive, and never even sees that "the world is shining around it." The nuns' idea of "nature" is not exactly created nature, and not exactly sinful nature. It seems closest to the idea of "conatus," a term first used by Stoic and Peripatetic philosophers of the classical world to describe the impulse to self-preservation that exists in all living things. For Spinoza in the seventeenth century, conatus is not an addition to a thing's other activities but "nothing but the actual essence of the thing."[2] To be at all, Spinoza says, a thing must be inclined to preserve itself. If you push away someone's hand when they try to poke your eye, or if you strive to increase your net worth, you're acting out of conatus. For many of the philosophers who use this concept, it is morally indifferent in itself. It is just the way living things behave, and could impel a person in a good or evil direction. "Nature" in *The Tree of Life* is self-preservation, a drive for self-enhancement. It is active, dominating.

The contrast of nature and grace in *The Tree of Life* is close to that of Thomas a Kempis:

> Nature indeed is wily and betrays many through its deceits and crafty ways, and has always self as its end. Nature always looks to its own advantage, considering what gain it can derive from another. But grace is not concerned with its own profit, but with what may benefit others. Nature is greedy and gladly takes rather than gives, and clings possessively to private possessions. But grace is kind and unselfish, avoids self-interest, is content with little, and rightly judges that it is more blessed to give than to receive. Grace seeks comfort only in God, finding delight in the Sovereign Good beyond all things visible.[3]

---

2. Spinoza, *Ethics* (Hertforshire, UK: Wordsworth, 2001), 3.7.

3. Thomas, *Imitation of Christ*, 3.54, accessed at http://www.ccel.org/ccel/kempis/imitation.THREE.3.html. Several blog commentators on the film have pointed to this connection. See Christopher Page, "The Tree of Life #19," at http://inaspaciousplace.wordpress.com/2011/08/20/the-tree-of-life-19-the-terrence-malick-vision-of-nature-and-grace/.

During Mrs. O'Brien's brief discourse on nature and grace, we move from scenes of her childhood to scenes of her as an adult swinging, running, playing in the street with her boys. Her playfulness, gracefulness, sheer mobility all testify that she lives by the way of grace. Contrary to what we might understand from the terms Malick uses, "grace" is not hostile to nature or indifferent to its beauty. The way of grace is, somewhat paradoxically, more attentive to nature than the way of nature. Mrs. O'Brien advises her sons, "The only way to be happy is to love. Unless you love, your life will flash by. Do good. Wonder. Hope. Help each other. Love everyone. Every leaf. Every ray of light. Forgive." She is playful, cheerful, smiling. When Mr. O'Brien goes out of town for a few weeks, the boys chase her around the house threateningly holding a lizard. She wakes her boys up by stuffing ice cubes in their tee shirts. The ethereal, not-quite-earthly Mother O'Brien embodies the way of grace.

Malick studied philosophy with Stanley Cavell at Harvard during the 1960s and completed a thesis on Martin Heidegger. Friends tell of Malick's pilgrimage to Germany, where he reportedly visited Heidegger in his forest cabin, though no one seems to know what they talked about and the reclusive Malick is not saying whether the two ever met at all.[4] Heidegger infuses much of *The Tree of Life*. Heidegger said that the great question of philosophy was, Why is there something rather than nothing? It is a question that expresses and evokes the wonder of Being, the awe we sometimes feel at the sheer fact of our own existence and the existence of anything. Most of the time, Heidegger claims, we don't consider the question of Being, the ontological question. We get so caught up with the specific things and gadgets that surround us, and we are concerned mostly with our immediate needs and the demands of life. We become obsessed with beings rather than with Being. We live in a state of forgetfulness. We are ontological amnesiacs, and what we have forgotten is the wonder of Being. Sometimes Being breaks in on us: A stunning sunset, an eagle in the sky or a snake upon a rock, a soul-stretching movement of a Beethoven *Quartet*, and at those moments the glory of Being breaks into our black-and-white lives in bright colors. In Heideggerian terms, the way of grace is the way of remembrance. Those who live by the way of grace live always with the remembrance of Being.

---

4. Several of Malick's college friends tell this story in Paul Maher, Jr., ed., *One Big Soul: An Oral History of Terrence Malick* (N.p.: Lulu, Kindle edition, 2012).

As soon as Mrs. O'Brien mentions nature, there is a cut to Mr. O'Brien and we hear his voice as he begins to pray over a dinner. Mr. O'Brien is nature. In Heideggerian terms, he is a man caught up with beings rather than Being. His advice to Jack always has to do with getting ahead, something that takes "fierce will." He's a perfectionist, or at least he admires perfectionists: "Toscanini once recorded a piece sixty-five times," he tells Jack as he turns hotdogs on the grill. "You know what he said when he finished? 'It could be better.' Think about it." He's a perfectionist with his lawn and garden.[5] Mr. O'Brien teaches Jack the proper way to pull weeds. He criticizes Jack at the dinner table for not putting the "runners" in right, and after R. L.'s death he remembers criticizing his dead son for the way he turned the pages of the music book as Mr. O'Brien played the piano. For Mr. O'Brien, creation is something to be tamed, controlled, dominated. He does not receive it as it is, but tries to mold it to his will. A man of nature, he wants a world without wrinkles and defects, and when it finds the world is not so, he tries to change it.

One manifestation of Mr. O'Brien's commitment to the way of nature is his control of language. One commentator on the film points to how he tries to control

> language utterly, so as to fit a framework of which he approves. For Pitt's father, do *not* call him "Dad," but "Father." He demands on being called "sir." He *cannot* be interrupted. He tells R. L. at one point at the dinner table, "Will you do me a favor? Do not speak unless you have something important to say," or to Jack, "Not one more *word* out of you." The way his children fight back, in his presence, is through disobeying his strictures of language. In the backyard while the father talks, Jack interrupts. "Don't interrupt!" Jack continues. "*Don't interrupt!*" "It's your house," Jack interrupts once more. "You can kick me out whenever you want," and then adds ominously, "You'd like to kill me."[6]

He controls Mrs. O'Brien's speech too. Family tensions roil around her, but he has trained her to sit quietly, registering her disapproval only by a look of worried reproach.

Heidegger, like many philosophers, puzzled over the question of time. Our ordinary ways of keeping time and thinking about time manifest our

5. We never actually see anything that the garden produces, but he sure pulls up a lot of weeds and damaged leaves of vegetables.

6. "Terrence Malick's Song of Himself," nilesfilmfiles.blogspot.com/2011/06/song-of-himself-terrence-malicks-tree.html, accessed February 25, 2013.

forgetfulness of Being. For us time is a line of points, the future out in the distance not yet here, the past "behind" us in the "no longer" and the present the fleeting knife-edge between the two. Heidegger thinks instead that the key to time is the recognition that human beings are hurtling toward death. Being human is, for Heidegger, "being-towards-death," and in that respect we are always outrunning our present moment. As Simon Critchley explains it, the human "always projects towards the future." Time can be understood only as a unity of the three "ecstasies" of past, present, and future.[7] In this respect too, the way of nature is an anti-Heideggerian way. Mr. O'Brien strives to master time. He marches through the plant where he works, pointing at his watch to a foreman. He tries to control the passing of time, and we shall see that he even tries to bring death itself under his dominion.

It doesn't work to his satisfaction, and one of the central dramas of the film is Mr. O'Brien's slow recognition that he has missed life by living in the way of nature. When he loses his job at the plant, he admits that he wanted to be loved for as a "great" man, "a Big Man." It was all taken away, and in pursuing his pathetic dreams of greatness he has been reduced to nothing. In the meantime, he missed life, missed everything that makes life grand and beautiful, missed the way of grace, "the glory around . . . trees, birds. I dishonored it all and didn't notice the glory." Those who lord over others don't succeed in their schemes, and when they fail they have nothing left but their shame. Shame is nature's final destination, and shame is the real legacy that Mr. O'Brien passes on to his sons. It's the aroma that fills the house, the shame of exclusion from the tree of life, which only comes in the way of grace.

Malick's presentation of the parents is not as schematic as I have made it sound. Mr. O'Brien lords it over his sons, but he also sprays them with the garden hose and plays games. In one telling sequence, Jack recounts his father's hypocrisies in a voice-over while the visuals show Mr. O'Brien horsing around with the boys in their bedroom. He is a man of nature, but he prays before meals and does his obeisances at church.[8] When the news comes that R. L. has been killed, we see him kneeling in earnest prayer. On the other side, Mrs. O'Brien's way of grace has limitations of its own. Mr. O'Brien goes on a business trip, leaving his wife in charge of the house. Absent Mr. O'Brien's commanding, intimating presence, the boys go wild. At

7. Critchley, "Heidegger's Being and Time, Part 8: Temporality," www.guardian.co.uk/commentisfree/belief/2009/jul/27/heidegger-being-time-philosophy.

8. Even his religion, though, has a "natural" feel to it. He wonders why he could have been such a failure when he never missed work and "tithed every Sunday." For the man of nature, religion is a contract in which God is obligated to reward dutiful performance.

first it is charming, but it becomes more threatening as time goes on. Mrs. O'Brien clearly has no way to control her boys. Jack's worst transgressions occur while the house is ruled—or not ruled—by the grace of his mother.

Jack is the battleground in the conflict between nature and grace. He comes to understand that he is an unstable amalgam of his parents. "Father, Mother. Always you wrestle inside me. Always you will." He admits that that Mr. O'Brien's orientation to "nature" is dominant. "I'm more like you than like her," he tells his father late in the film. And this inner conflict makes the adult Jack what he is. As an architect, he necessarily combines his mother's sensitivity to beauty with his father's determination to shape the world according to prescribed plans. He spends his life poring over blueprints, but it is only through the blueprints that he can produce something like the splendid glass tower where he works.

Some critics have suggested that Malick shares Heidegger's contempt for modern life. Anthony Lane suspects that "Malick finds something distasteful in our current mores," citing the mumbled dialog in Jack's architectural firm.[9] That may highlight a contradiction in Malick's outlook, or, more likely, suggests that nature and grace are not as polarized as Mrs. O'Brien makes them sound.

Malick is a famously "graced" filmmaker. "He loves to be surprised," says production designer Jack Fisk. "He's always looking for spontaneity." Malick makes few changes to the locations where he shoots.[10] Director of photography Emmanuel Lubezki describes filming the children of the film as a form of fishing: You wait for hours until you get a bite and reel in a winner. Some of the scenes were shot while the actors were unaware that the camera was rolling.[11] Fiona Shaw, who plays Mrs. O'Brien's mother, tells an interviewer that Malick is "the opposite of a director," a filmmaker who lets his actors create scenes and characters along with him. He's always looking for "accidents to happen."[12] Malick the filmmaker films in the way of grace, taking whatever comes, looking in every nook and cranny for the glory that smiles through everything. Heideggerian that he apparently is, he films

9. Lane, "Time Trip," *The New Yorker*, May 30, 2011, available at www.newyorker.com/arts/critics/cinema/2011/05/30/110530crci_cinema_lane.

10. Bill Desowitz, "Immersed in Movies: Jack Fisk Climbs the Tree of Life," http://blogs.indiewire.com/thompsononhollywood/jack-fisk-climbs-the-tree-of-life.

11. Bob Fisher, "Sights Unseen," http://www.icgmagazine.com/wordpress/2011/05/11/sights-unseen.

12. Helen O'Hara, "Fiona Shaw Talks *Tree of Life*," http://www.empireonline.com/interviews/interview.asp?IID=1255.

beings in expectation that Being might erupt at any moment. At the same time, Malick hired consultants to produce the special effects that make up the eighteen-minute evolution sequence at the center of the film. They kept redoing effects until he liked what he saw. At the end of the day, someone had to edit the miles and miles of film, and as director Malick insisted that it was not done until he was pleased with it.[13] The initial cut of *Tree of Life* was eight hours long, and Malick is said to be working on a six-hour version. Even so, most of the film he took doesn't end up on the screen. The "graced" camera that just takes what comes only can produce the beauty of *The Tree of Life* only if Malick is willing to act like a man of nature and slice it into pieces.

But the biggest complication of Mrs. O'Brien's nature/grace scheme has to do with the last promise that Mrs. O'Brien remembers from the nuns: "They told us that those who live in the way of grace never come to a bad end." As she says these words, the camera moves in on R. L. Of the O'Brien boys, he is the embodiment of the way of grace, and yet he is also the one who dies young, the one who comes to a bad end. The film challenges the nuns' simplistic outlook on the world. What kind of world has Malick brought us to, where graceful boys come to bad ends?

This is another point at which some suggest Malick is a "dualist" or a Gnostic. In a strict sense, as I've argued in an earlier chapter, the second charge makes no sense. Gnostics believed that the physical creation was an unfortunate mistake. Malick, by contrast, is thunderstruck at the beauty around him. He views the physical creation as a magical country. "Dualist" may be closer to the truth. In Malick's previous film, *The Thin Red Line*, Witt ponders whether "not one power but two" rules the universe. How else can you explain the combination of wonder and horror that makes up this world? Death and evil are everywhere, so insistently present that they must somehow be written into the fabric of things. That is not the answer that the film gives to the questions the discourse on nature and grace raises. But it is the right question, a question that Malick poses from his first invocation of the Book of Job. And it is a question that can only be answered from the point of view of the end, not only the end of this particular story but the end of time.

---

13. Some reports indicate that Malick spent two to three years editing the film.

Chapter 7

Windows and Doors

"Close the door quietly. Fifty times."

—Mr. O'Brien

THE TREE OF LIFE begins at a window, an open window. A young Mrs. O'Brien looks out smiling from a barn window, the shutter swings and her air dances in the breeze, as the adult Mrs. O'Brien talks in a voice-over about the way of grace that recognizes the glory shining through everything. From the first moment, windows are linked with grace. Windows symbolize the receptivity of a graced person to the glory that shines through everything.[1] If we wished to press the symbol theologically, we might say that a window represents receptivity to the Light of God and the wind of his Spirit.

Through the rest of the film, the camera often focuses on windows, openings to light and air.[2] The windows of the O'Brien's home are curtained, but the light streams in, veiled. Mrs. O'Brien puts her infant boys in cradles next to the window, with the curtain draped so that the child is exposed to the direct light and breeze. Mr. O'Brien holds young R. L., patting him on the back and gazing out the window. Though he is more associated with nature than grace, Mr. O'Brien here enjoys a graced moment, open to the glory of sun and wind, the glory of a newborn child. (His look of rapt wonder at the feet of his newborn son is a similar moment of glory.) Mrs. O'Brien plays with young Jack by hiding herself in the curtains, and

1. Thanks to Toby Sumpter and Jeff Meyers for insight on the symbolism of windows in the film.

2. This is partly a technical necessity. Malick used natural light throughout the film, rather than lighting scenes artificially. Scenes take place near windows to allow light in.

thereby becomes the embodiment of veiled glory. A woman covers R. L.'s face and kisses him through the curtain. Glory comes veiled, but it is there for those open to receive it.

This image takes several ironic twists in the course of the film. Mrs. O'Brien receives the telegram about R. L.'s death while living in a fashionable home with a large plate glass window in the back, looking over a large green lawn. The room is filled with natural light, glory is shining everywhere, and then Mrs. O'Brien reads of her son's death and collapses to the floor with a suppressed cry. Can glory shine through, even when one who lives by grace *does* come to a bad end? As the film moves through scenes of mourning and comfort in the minutes that follow, Malick gives us one of the most memorable visual images of the film: The camera looks up a tower in a church, showing us a corkscrew of stained glass leading to a shining circular center. Light shines white through the top window, but it is refracted in blues, greens, reds, and yellows of the stained glass. While this image is shown, we hear the sounds of a funeral—an organ, greetings from well-wishers, assurances from a pastor. The juxtaposition doesn't solve the problem of R. L.'s death. It intensifies it: What kind of world is it that includes both such splendors and such abject loss?

As a boy, Jack looks for glory. He prays a charmingly boyish prayer that includes a petition that God would prevent him from "getting dogs in fights." On the playground at school, we hear his voice-over questions, "Where do you live? I want to know what you are. I want to see what you see." After a boy drowns in the swimming pool, though, Jack goes through a period of adolescent nihilism: "Why should I be good when you're not?" he asks God. He begins hanging out with the rough boys from the neighborhood, and he becomes their leader. His main act of destruction is, significantly, to break out the windows of a neighbor's garage.

It's a scene fraught with Augustinian allusions. In a famous scene in Book 2 of *Confessions*, Augustine describes how as a young boy he participated in the theft of some pears from a nearby orchard.

> Theft is punished by thy law, O Lord, and by the law written in men's hearts, which not even ingrained wickedness can erase. For what thief will tolerate another thief stealing from him? Even a rich thief will not tolerate a poor thief who is driven to theft by want. Yet I had a desire to commit robbery, and did so, compelled to it by neither hunger nor poverty, but through a contempt for well-doing and a strong impulse to iniquity. For I pilfered something which I already had in sufficient measure, and of much better quality. I did

45

not desire to enjoy what I stole, but only the theft and the sin itself. There was a pear tree close to our own vineyard, heavily laden with fruit, which was not tempting either for its color or for its flavor. Late one night—having prolonged our games in the streets until then, as our bad habit was—a group of young scoundrels, and I among them, went to shake and rob this tree. We carried off a huge load of pears, not to eat ourselves, but to dump out to the hogs, after barely tasting some of them ourselves. Doing this pleased us all the more because it was forbidden.[3]

This small crime becomes a source for Augustine's meditations on the nature of sin.

Those pears that we stole were fair to the sight because they were thy creation, O Beauty beyond compare, O Creator of all, O thou good God—God the highest good and my true good. Those pears were truly pleasant to the sight, but it was not for them that my miserable soul lusted, for I had an abundance of better pears. I stole those simply that I might steal, for, having stolen them, I threw them away. My sole gratification in them was my own sin, which I was pleased to enjoy; for, if any one of these pears entered my mouth, the only good flavor it had was my sin in eating it. And now, O Lord my God, I ask what it was in that theft of mine that caused me such delight; for behold it had no beauty of its own— certainly not the sort of beauty that exists in justice and wisdom, nor such as is in the mind, memory senses, and the animal life of man; nor yet the kind that is the glory and beauty of the stars in their courses; nor the beauty of the earth, or the sea—teeming with spawning life, replacing in birth that which dies and decays. Indeed, it did not have that false and shadowy beauty which attends the deceptions of vice.[4]

Augustine realizes in retrospect that he would never have participated in the theft except for the pressure of his peers. Sin has a social dimension; camaraderie in wrongdoing reduces resistance to wrongdoing. Augustine also remembers that the pears were not particularly good, and that better pears were readily and legally available. The theft was a pure act of sin. It was not motivated by a desire for something good, but arose from the sheer joy of sinning. For Augustine, the profundity of human evil is evident in the fact that we take delight in sin's very destructiveness. As he summarizes,

3. Augustine, *Confessions*, trans. Albert Outler (Mineola, NY: Dover Thrift Editions), 2.4

4. Ibid., 2.6

"the pleasure I got was not from the pears, it was in the crime itself, enhanced by the companionship of my fellow sinners."[5]

Jack certainly delights in his vandalism. Another boy suggests breaking the windows, but Jack is the first to do it, and afterwards he adopts an awkward posture that combines embarrassment and pride, as he looks to his friends for approval. They approve, and he takes up another stone. Given the imagery of windows in the film, this is not merely destructiveness but a choice of a particular path of life. He is no longer looking for the windows that let the glory in. Because he doubts God's goodness, he shatters the windows and closes himself off from the light. As we will see in a later chapter, he eventually realizes that he has closed himself off, and he begins to look for a way back.

The adult Jack lives in a clean, white, uncluttered house with windows everywhere. Yet from our first glimpse of his gray, drawn face we know that he does not see the glory, that he turns a frown toward the love that smiles through all things. It's not because the light isn't shining in. The flame is still dancing on his walls, dancing all around him. God is still there in the disguise of trees, sun, clouds, birds. Jack works in a skyscraper that is made of glass, but the windows filter the natural light and often create dim interior spaces. He has shut out the glory. He's still twelve years old, breaking windows.

Doorways mark transitions from one place or state to another. Jack's birth is a swim through a doorway, and his sexual awakening involves passing through another doorway. Joe McCulloch writes that Jack's "stirring sexuality lead[s] him to covertly enter a neighboring woman's unlocked home to wander around: a terrific metaphor for sexual fantasy—invasive without risking physical notice—though Malick keeps building and building his scene until the lad is pulling scanty things out of the bedroom drawers and rubbing them."[6] Jack's teenage conflict with his father centers on doorways. Mr. O'Brien enters the boys' bedroom to wake them with a crash, and when he leaves the house for work he bursts through the screen door. It's an expression of the "fierce will" of the way of nature, the fierce will that is necessary to get ahead in the world. When Jack wakes him from an afternoon nap by letting the screen door slam, Mr. O'Brien demands that he learn to open doors more quietly, furtively. He stands him at the

5. Ibid., 2.8

6. McCulloch, "Terrence Malick's 'The Tree of Life': A Few Thoughts Subsequent to a Local Screening Sponsored by a College's Theology Department," http://mubi.com/notebook/posts/terrence-malicks-the-tree-of-life-a-few-thoughts-subsequent-to-a-local-screening-sponsored-by-a-colleges-theology-department.

screen door and demands that he close it "quietly, fifty times," counting as he goes. Mr. O'Brien's hypocrisy with regard to the door is a symbol of his more general hypocrisy. Because he is a man of nature who wants everyone to please him, he doesn't even recognize that he imposes standards on Jack that he doesn't hold to himself.

The main doorway image of the film is one that we have discussed above. Wandering through the desert, the adult Jack encounters an isolated door frame. There is no room on either side of the door, but to move ahead he has to pass through the door. It marks a change from one state to the other, from a state of depression brought on by his adherence to nature to an embrace of the state of grace. It's a doorway, but once he passes through he is prepared to open the windows, to let the light shine through, and to be warmed by the glory that smiles through all things.

Chapter 8

Trees, Birds, Everything

"Love everything. Love every leaf, every drop of rain."

——Mrs. O'Brien

The Tree of Life is a gorgeous film, with scenes of nature worthy of David Attenborough's *Planet Earth*. There are lingering shots of sunflowers and irises, towering and flowering trees, rivers running between thick green banks. In one unforgettable scene, which reportedly happened spontaneously,[1] Mrs. O'Brien catches a butterfly on her finger. Later she sits on the curb stroking the butterfly's wings, as a curious cat looks on. One long scene follows a shape-shifting cloud of birds as it moves over a cityscape at twilight.[2] Most of the film's nature scenes occur during the evolution sequence in the first half of the film. Nature is depicted in all its variety. Volcanoes boom, hot springs hiss from rock, ocean waves surge and lap. Jellyfish undulate mesmerizingly toward the camera. The lush-

---

1. One of the crew members describes the incident: "We were getting ready for a morning scene outside between Jessica (Chastain) and Brad (Pitt). . . . The actors were rehearsing their lines in full wardrobe and ready to roll, when Terry suddenly noticed a butterfly. It wasn't uncommon for him to get excited over things like a bird perched on a tree branch and want to film them. So we followed the butterfly through three blocks of Smithville. Jessica gracefully stepped out into the middle of the street, backlit by the morning sun. She held her hand out and the butterfly came full circle and landed directly on it. It stayed there for some time. We were joking around afterwards that everyone is going to think it's a CG effect, but rest assured, it's a real butterfly, and [director of photography] Chivo [Lubezki] got it all on film." (Bob Fisher, "Sights Unseen," http://www.icgmagazine.com/wordpress/2011/05/11/sights-unseen/.)

2. Perhaps that one was computer generated, but no matter: it works.

ness of the primordial forest in the dinosaur scenes is astonishing. Even when the camera is not focused on natural phenomena, they are intensely present. The live oak trees that line the Waco street where the O'Briens live are wondrous with hanging tangles of Spanish moss and their knots of branches. Sunlight immerses many scenes.

Malick loves natural beauty and sublimity, but the nature scenes of the film are not merely window dressing. They are integral to the film's purpose and "message" about nature and grace. Those who live self-centeredly in the way of nature ignore the glory that shines around them. It is a divine glory, but it shines through the natural world. Mr. O'Brien's incessant efforts to improve on the natural world—working the yard, pulling weeks in the garden—reveal his tendency toward the way of nature. He finds things to complain about in the world around him, rather than contemplating its splendors. Malick's camera meanwhile seduces us into the way of grace. We can only avoid seeing it if we close our eyes, and even then the beauty of the music will still come through. We ponder how Mr. O'Brien's life would have been different if he had had a chance to view the film that he is in.

Of course, the nature scenes also underscore the Joban themes of the film. As we have already noted, Malick follows Job in the way he answers Mrs. O'Brien's "Why?" The Lord's answer to Job is to remind him of the wonders of his creation, and Malick's is the same. "Where were you?" Mrs. O'Brien asks, and God answers by displaying the glory and asking "Where were you when I laid the foundation of the earth?" Creation's glory does not provide a neat intellectual response to the problem of evil. Malick is not saying that evil is the chiaroscuro that gives the world's beauty its depth and richness, nor is Job. Creation is not a neat intellectual answer because we don't respond to evil mainly in the way of intellect. Argument is not the answer to evil. Love is. Glory is.

The title *The Tree of Life* puts us immediately into the biblical world. The Bible begins with humanity in a garden, full of all good things, at the center of which is the tree of life. No explanation is given of the tree, but the Lord's statement after the fall of Adam suggests that the tree of life was somehow capable of communicating eternal life: "Behold, the man has become like one of us, knowing good and evil; and now, he might stretch out his hand and take also from the tree of life, and eat, and live forever" (Gen 3:22). To prevent this, the Lord sends Adam and Eve out of Eden, and stations cherubim with flaming swords at the gate to prevent their re-entry. A tree of life is precisely what man has lost: The available abundance of Eden, harmony between God and humanity and between man and woman, life abundant and rich. Though the fall takes place at the tree of knowledge of good and evil, "tree of life" is the abyss of absence, a sign of the world we have lost. It is the glow of innocence and childhood in the receding past.

Through most of the Bible, the tree of life remains inaccessible. A few times in Proverbs, Solomon tells us that some phenomenon in the world is like a recovery of the tree of life. The righteous man of Psalm 1 is a fruitful tree, and in the Proverbs wisdom is a tree of life to those who find her (Prov 3:18). The fruit of the righteous is a tree of life (11:30), as is a desire fulfilled (13:12). It's not until we get to the very end of the Bible, to the Revelation of St. John, that the tree of life makes a strong reappearance. Jesus promises the fruit of the tree of life in Paradise to those who gain victory with him by suffering witness (Rev 2:7), and in the final vision of the New Jerusalem that descends from heaven, the single Edenic tree of life has multiplied into a grove of trees. Trees of life line the river of life that flows through the center of the city, each tree bears twelve fruits, and even the leaves are therapeutic, given for the healing of the nations (Rev 22:1–2, 14, 19). What was lost in Eden is recovered in the eschaton, and more is found at the end than was available at the beginning.

Malick's film rings the changes on this biblical theme in a variety of ways. The overall structure of the film mimics the biblical narrative. Jack's childhood estrangement from God, his parents, and his brother and his eventual reconciliation with them draw the arc for his life as a whole. In the smaller story, he wanders from Eden because of the death of a boy, and in the larger arc of his life he spends much of his adulthood wandering in the path of nature, wondering where he took a wrong step. By the end of the film, he glimpses the final reconciliation of all things, and he is able to relax, smile at the world, and see again the glory shining through everything. He loses the tree of life, but in the film he recovers it.

Actual trees recur again and again in the film. Early in the second half of the movie, Mr. O'Brien plants a tree while young Jack stands watching. As the two water the tree, Mrs. O'Brien says "You'll be tall before the tree is grown." Jack is himself a tree, watered by his parents, growing toward the sky, which is where his mother says God lives. Jack walks through the neighborhood swinging a dead stick, a fragment of a tree that makes Jack a tree himself.[3] One of the trees in the backyard of the O'Brien home

---

3. A point made in the review at "Terrence Malick's Song of Himself," http://niles-filmfiles. blogspot.com/2011/06/song-of-himself-terrence-malicks-tree.html.

becomes the center of the boys' world. They swing from ropes tied to its branches, and they climb steps nailed to the trunk. At the top of the ladder, though, there is no tree house. The tree leads to the sky, as a number of the shots emphasize by following the trunk up to the top branches and beyond to the blue sky and clouds. Trees are ladders connecting heaven and earth. For Jack, Mrs. O'Brien and R. L. are trees of life who led Jack to the door of God's house in the sky, gave him life, showed him the glory of living in the way of grace. When he wanders from them, he wanders from God, because he is wandering from the ones who could bring him back to God's door. If he is going to get back to God, he needs to find the trees to climb to heaven.

Other images echo the tree-ladder image. Ladders stretch upward, stairs lead up to rooms illuminated by bright light through windows. Jack is constantly moving up and down on the elevator during his day at work. This is linked to the frequent appearance of birds in the film. The sound of gulls is one of the first things we hear in the film, and in other scenes, including the last one, we hear birds chirping and singing. A cloud of birds makes shapes in the sky over the city where the adult Jack works. Birds ascend toward God's home. They sing like the morning stars that greeted the dawn of creation. Ladders to heaven evoke another biblical character and incident, Jacob's dream at Bethel (Gen 28), in which he saw angels descending and ascending on a ziggurat connecting earth to heaven. Jack is a Job; he is also Jacob: *JackO'*Brien.[4]

The up-and-down of trees and ladders is imaged again in airplanes, which figure importantly into several scenes of the film. As with most of the symbols of the film, this one has two sides. Mr. O'Brien is waiting for a flight when he receives news of R. L.'s death. When we first see him, he is waving his hand in the air, directing the pilot or some other crew member. He other hand holds a phone to his ear. The drone of the propellers drowns out his words, but we can see the horrified shock of his face. We can read his incredulous "What?" shouted into the phone, and then he stares silently listening, his mouth incapable of forming the words.

For Mr. O'Brien, airplanes are tools that help him achieve his ambitions. Planes are there to be managed and controlled and directed, like the men he manages at the plant. When he returns from a long international business trip, he shows off his Pan American Airlines ticket, and boasts of the stainless steel bathrooms on the plane. His imagination is drawn to metals, to machines. He tells Mrs. O'Brien that the deal seems to be going

4. Ibid.

through, and adds, "If it doesn't, to hell with them." As with everything, Mr. O'Brien wants the airplane to do his bidding, to serve his purposes. He doesn't give a second thought to the fact that his plane flight took him nearer to heaven, and joined him with the birds and brought him close to the singing stars.

Mrs. O'Brien also rides in a plane. She is tucking the boys in, and R. L. asks her to "tell a story from before we can remember." Back in the distant past was a time when Mrs. O'Brien ascended to the heavens. It was a graduation present, and for several minutes we are with her in a small yellow plane—a mechanical canary—dipping and turning like a bird in flight. Fields and forests appear vertiginously below and the sun blazes on the horizon. At one point, the plane turns upside down, and then it shoots straight up in the sky. Mrs. O'Brien has nothing to gain from the ride, no agenda or use. The plane is not a tool to advance her own purposes, but a source of sheer delight, a way for her to mingle with the clouds and the birds that are closer to God's home in the sky. She rides a plane because it enables her to see glory, the expanse of love that smiles through everything, a smile as wide as the horizon.

During the scenes of her plane ride, we hear Jack's whispered prayers or wishes: "Mother, make me good, brave." She can do it, because in the next scene Mrs. O'Brien herself takes flight. She dances for Jack when he was a toddler. He bangs away and she spins and jumps in rhythm. But after the plane flight she dances in the air. Jack can fly with the birds toward the home of God because his mother will take him there. She is a mediator of God's presence and glory to her sons. She is a tree of life. She is one of the morning stars singing at the birth of creation, and at its rebirth.

Grass and weeds add further texture and variety to the natural symbolism of the film. In several scenes, we see tufts of water grass waves under water. Moist in their boyish innocence, the O'Briens play in the meadow, roll in the grass, pick up rocks, and discover discarded dog bones, which Jack says is a dinosaur bone. R. L. stands in the reeds beside a river, and runs his hand through the tall grass as he walks through a field. Remembering the time when grass was a playground, the adult Jack runs his hand through the small patch of grass outside his office building. For Mr. O'Brien, grass is not a playground, not part of the glory that shines everywhere, but instead part of the natural world that needs to be tamed. He sends Jack to work in the yard, pulling weeds, making sure that the lawn is watered, demanding to know if the "runners" have been put in. He spends time in the garden pulling weeds and trying to bring order to the wild greenery that grows there.

If trees portray human beings in one aspect, so does grass. "All flesh is grass," Isaiah says (40:6), and "its loveliness like the flower of the field." In the Bible, grass is a reminder of the brevity of life. "My days are a lengthened shadow, and I wither like the grass" (Ps 102:11), and the following Psalm adds "as for man, his days are like grass; as a flower of the field, so he flourishes. When the wind has passed over it, it is no more" (Ps 103:15–16). In some psalms, grass is part of an answer to the problem of evil. The wicked flourish; they seem to sprout up everywhere, like grass. But like grass, we are assured, they won't last (Pss 37:2; 92:7). It is a sobering thought, but for scripture not depressing. Even though the grass lasts only a moment, God dresses it with glory greater than Solomon's (Matt 6:29–30). Even though it withered in the sun, still love and glory shine through it.

Malick makes use of the biblical imagery of trees, grass, and fruit, of trees as ladders, but there is a biological dimension to this image as well. Lamarck was the first to use a tree to explain the relationships between different species of animals, and in his *Origin of Species*, Darwin also suggested the image of a tree to describe the development of species from an ancestor:

> The affinities of all the beings of the same class have sometimes been represented by a great tree. I believe this simile largely speaks the truth. The green and budding twigs may represent existing species; and those produced during former years may represent the long succession of extinct species. At each period of growth all the growing twigs have tried to branch out on all sides, and to overtop and kill the surrounding twigs and branches, in the same manner as species and groups of species have at all times overmastered other species in the great battle for life. The limbs divided into great branches, and these into lesser and lesser branches, were themselves once, when the tree was young, budding twigs; and this connection of the former and present buds by ramifying branches may well represent the classification of all extinct and living species in groups subordinate to groups. Of the many twigs which flourished when the tree was a mere bush, only two or three, now grown into great branches, yet survive and bear the other branches; so with the species which lived during long-past geological periods, very few have left living and modified descendants. From the first growth of the tree, many a limb and branch has decayed and dropped off; and these fallen branches of various sizes may represent those whole orders, families, and genera

which have now no living representatives, and which are known to us only in a fossil state. As we here and there see a thin straggling branch springing from a fork low down in a tree, and which by some chance has been favoured and is still alive on its summit, so we occasionally see an animal like the Ornithorhynchus or Lepidosiren, which in some small degree connects by its affinities two large branches of life, and which has apparently been saved from fatal competition by having inhabited a protected station. As buds give rise by growth to fresh buds, and these, if vigorous, branch out and overtop on all sides many a feebler branch, so by generation I believe it has been with the great Tree of Life, which fills with its dead and broken branches the crust of the earth, and covers the surface with its ever-branching and beautiful ramifications.[5]

In biology, the tree of life portrays the interrelationships of the creatures of earth. The trunk of the tree moves upward from amoeba to worms to acranial animals and fish, to primitive mammals and apes and finally to man, nested in the topmost branches. From the trunk the various subgenuses branch off, beasts of prey on one side of the mammal section of the tree, hoofed animals and whales branching on the other side. If the tree had not grown amoeba, there would never have been more complex invertebrates, and without invertebrates there never would have been vertebrates or mammals. Just as upper branches and fruit depend on the trunk, so the greater animals depend on the lesser.

Malick uses the biological image of a tree of life partly to emphasize this interdependence, but when we recognize that he combines the biblical and biological associations of the tree of life we can see another theme emerging. As Darwin describes it, the tree of life is a tree of competition. Each species strives along the way of nature to ensure its own survival, whether or not they trample other species along the way. The tree of life has many dead branches, and the ground beneath is littered with the detritus of natural selection.

By combining the evolutionary tree with the biblical one, Malick points to a way of life that transcends nature and the competition for survival. Several times we see the boys climbing toward the top of the tree of life. They are growing to become the highest form of being, which is man, but the tree is also a ladder that leads to the sky where God is. Evolution and religion are not opposed to one another in Malick's vision; rather, growing large enough to penetrate the sky in order to know God is the highest peak

5. Darwin, *Origin of Species* (London: Grant Richards, 1902), 117–18.

of evolutionary development. There is plenty of "nature red in tooth and claw" in the film—circling hammerheads, an injured Plesiosaurus, blood in the water, but evolution itself flowers in the way of grace. Compassion is a higher stage of evolution than survival, as the way of grace transcends the way of nature.

Chapter 9

Hands

"He's in God's hands now."

──Minister to Mrs. O'Brien

THE MINSTER'S WORDS TO the grieving Mrs. O'Brien contain the film's first reference to hands. It is supposed to be reassuring. R. L. has gone to be with God. He is no longer vulnerable, no longer in danger. He is safe in the mighty hands of God.

Mrs. O'Brien is not reassured. She responds with a plaintive, "He was in God's hands the whole time, wasn't he?"

Her question doesn't arise from doubt. If God isn't, then there is no question. A belief in the odd randomness of the world in some ways dilutes the question of suffering. If "shit happens," then there's nothing much more to say about it. Mrs. O'Brien's question assumes that there is a God and that he is good. If R. L. was in God's hands from the beginning, in God's hands before he knew he was in God's hands, why did he die? Can death pluck a good boy, a boy walking in the way of grace, from God's hands? Is death stronger than God? Job's protests are passionate because he expects God to do him fair. Mrs. O'Brien's anguish comes from the same source. If there is a good God, a God with hands to hold boys, then suffering seems utterly inexplicable. Faith doesn't ease questions of suffering. Faith intensifies them.

But the hands we see in *The Tree of Life* are not the hands of God. We see instead human hands, and we see them a lot. Within the first two minutes of the film, the camera has focused on the young Mrs. O'Brien's hands grasping the sill of a barn window as she gazes in wonder at the world around her. Her hands reach out through the window as if to grasp the glory that shines through. She reaches out to the wind as if hoping to hold it in her hand. She holds a goat in her arms, and holds out her hand toward grazing cows, turning it over and over in the breeze. A man, presumably her father, comes near her and stretches out his hand to touch her shoulder and then hug her. He picks her up, and the camera moves to focus on her hand laying on her father's shoulder. When we skip ahead to Mrs. O'Brien as an adult, she reaches to pull teenage Jack up from the ground, a scene that will later be replicated when she bends over an open grave to help someone out. Hands protect, hands open to receive glory, hands help.

As Mrs. O'Brien wanders weeping and aimless down the middle of the street, her husband catches up to her and lays a comforting hand on her shoulder. Mr. O'Brien has skilled hands. He plays Bach's *Toccata and Fugue in D Minor* on the organ, plays the piano well, and swings his hands rhythmically to conduct. R. L. is able to join hands with his father, harmonizing on the guitar as his father plays the piano. After Mr. O'Brien scolds Jack for interrupting at the table, Mrs. O'Brien reassures him with a touch to the shoulder. Hands express compassion, and not only when placed on the shoulder. After Mrs. O'Brien's exchange with the minister about the hands of God, Malick cuts to a closeup of two huge black hands, holding Mrs. O'Brien's in hers. These are not God's hands, yet they are. God's comforting, protective presence comes to Mrs. O'Brien through the hands of her friends. The hands of her friends are God's hands to her.

Late in the film, R. L. signals his forgiveness of Jack by touching his hands, then his shoulder, then his head, repeating the gesture of confirmation that was shown only minutes earlier. "What was it you showed me?" Jack asks. "I didn't know how to name you then. But I see it was you. Always you were calling me." Named or not, Jack knows what R. L. means. A moment later, Jack is stomping down the street on tin-can stilts. He stops and lets a neighbor boy play with them, the boy whose head was burned in a house fire. As the boy straps on the stilts, Jack passes on R. L.'s gesture, laying a hand on the boy's shoulder. The boy has been a symbol of God's capriciousness or cruelty: "You'll let anything happen," Jack complains in prayer when he thinks about the fire. By laying his hand on the boy's shoulder, Jack shows that he has been brought to the way of Alyosha Karamazov, who, unlike his brother Ivan, doesn't compile a catalogue of suffering to construct a case against God, but instead embraces the hurting, kisses his brother, and waters the earth with his tears.

The evolution sequence in the first half of the film culminates in several scenes of dinosaurs. A pleiosaurus lies on a beach, and the camera moves to show us a huge bloody gash in his side. The scene cuts to hammerhead sharks circling menacingly in bloody water. Nature is red in tooth and claw. A few moments later, a much smaller dinosaur in a verdant forest hesitatingly checks the wind, listens to the threatening sounds that echo through the woods, carefully moves forward. This is not a safe world. It is the world of nature that lives by the way of nature.

But that leads to a third dinosaur scene. A predator comes out of the woods and splashes across a shallow river. In the foreground we see a smaller dinosaur lying on the pebbles beside the river. He is breathing heavily, weak, perhaps dying. The predator comes to his side and peers at him. As the prostrate dinosaur begins to raise his head, the other presses his head down with one of his feet and makes a threatening sound. We expect him to take advantage of weakness, but he doesn't. Instead, having pressed the injured dinosaur to the ground, he pads away and splashes down the river. It is a birth of compassion, emerging within the evolutionary sequence. The last shot in the evolution sequence shows a meteor hit the ocean, sending tsumani waves across the globe. It is perhaps the meteor that some scientists believe wiped out primitive life on earth, making way for man. When compassion has evolved, the world is ready for the climax of creation, a creature with hands.

When the evolution sequence began, Lacrimosa from Zbigniew Preisner's *Requiem for a Friend* fills the universe. Lamentation echoes through the galaxies, and, as we have seen, the evolution sequence is the Joban answer to that lament. After the first few moments, the music fades out and through most of the evolution sequence, we hear only crashes and rumbles and the hiss of steam as waves crash against cooling lava. As soon as we see an expression of animal compassion, the voice-over returns: "Light of my life. I search for you. I hope." Music returns, not the *Lacrimosa*, but the Amen from the *Agnus Dei* of Berlioz's *Requiem*. It plays only for a few seconds, but it marks a shift. Creation, and especially the evolution of compassion, has answered the "Why?" and the "Where were you?" It is enough, as the chorus pronounces an Amen to a world where glory shines through everything and where velociraptors might pity their prey.

Every theme in *The Tree of Life* is cut through by the nature/grace dualism that opens the film. Hands can be used to express comfort, compassion, sympathy, and forgiveness, but they can also be used to express control and to inflict pain. Jack's great sin against R. L. injures the latter's hand. Several times in the film, Mr. O'Brien leads a reluctant Jack around the yard, holding him by the arm, showing him all the places where Jack has failed to make the yard flourish. In one scene, Mr. O'Brien doesn't even speak. Pulling Jack behind him, he points to the flaws in the grass and grunts: "Huh. Huh. Huh." Jack turns and hugs him, but Mr. O'Brien stiffens and turns away in embarrassment. While Mr. O'Brien gives Jack advice about pursuing his dreams, he holds his son's shoulder, fairly dragging Jack along. Mr. O'Brien's hand doesn't guide a willing disciple but forces an unwilling one to go in a direction that he doesn't want to go. In a tense scene between Jack and Mr. O'Brien, Jack says, "You'd like to kill me." Mr. O'Brien takes him roughly by the neck and glares at him with an enraged stare. Mr. O'Brien's games with the boys are designed to teach them to use their hands to fight. He plays slap-hands on the sofa in the living room, and tries to get Jack and R. L. to punch him in the jaw.

Mr. O'Brien is not an unfeeling ogre. He hugs the boys, asks that they hug him. Almost always, though, they are stiff and unresponsive. After the funeral of the drowned boy, Mr. O'Brien tries to pull his boys close to comfort them, but Jack and R. L. pull away to do somersaults in the church yard. Mr. O'Brien stands alone for a moment, and then forces Steve, the youngest son, close to him. Even when he expresses affection, he is a man of nature, trying to get his own way, lording it over the boys.

In his career, Mr. O'Brien uses his hands to grab and take. His hands are not open but closed into fists to fight or to hold on to whatever he can get. We see him playing cards, looking fearful and disappointed when his hands don't bring money into his hands. In one scene, Mr. O'Brien drives the boys through the rich neighborhood, offering his cynical commentary on the wealthy. Joe McCulloch calls attention to the sequence of the scenes:

> Brad Pitt as the story's demanding ur-father, voicing his insecurities over the downtrodden economic state of his family, is immediately followed by a scene of the clan purchasing foodstuffs from an obviously less-advantaged black marketplace, groups of race-divided children staring at each other without commingling, followed by a scene of Jessica Chastain as a blessed Mother doing chores on a rather comfortable lawn.[1]

1. McCulloch, "Terrence Malick's 'The Tree of Life': A Few Thoughts Subsequent to a Local Screening Sponsored by a College's Theology Department," http://mubi.com/notebook/posts/terrence-malicks-the-tree-of-life-a-few-thoughts-subsequent-to-a-local-screening-sponsored-by-a-colleges-theology-department.

Mr. O'Brien is sullenly embittered at his lot in life, but though he owns less than half the real estate in town, and though he doesn't seem a good card player, he is able to provide a comfortable life for his family. The way of nature, though, leaves him discontented. His hands are never full enough, never able to grab everything he wants or everything he thinks he deserves. During a car ride, one of the boys has his hand out the window playing with the passing breeze like his mother in the opening scene of the film. He is more concerned with feeling the wind through his fingers than he is with filling his hands with winnings.[2]

In the closing scenes of the film, release and reconciliation are symbolized by the hands. Flanked by two women, Mrs. O'Brien raises her hands to the sky and opens them, saying "I give you my son." Like Abraham, she is willing to give up even her dearest possession. As Berlioz's *Agnus Dei* comes to a crescendo, Mrs. O'Brien kisses an aging, liver-spotted hand, and turns it young again. By the end of the film, even Mr. O'Brien's hands have been restored. When he has been humbled and begins to see the glory he has been ignoring, he confesses his failures to Jack and lays a gentle hand on Jack's shoulder. It is the first gentle touch from Mr. O'Brien. He has evolved from nature to grace, and his hands can unclench to become hands of compassion, hands of grace, the hands of God.

2. This gesture also seems to resonate with themes of Ecclesiastes and other wisdom literature, which indicates that wealth is as evanescent as wind.

Chapter 10

Memory

"Tell us a story from before we can remember."

—R. L. O'Brien

Adult Jack is haunted by memories of his childhood, especially memories of his brother. When we first see him, he is getting out of bed. He hesitates, starts to go back to bed, and then gets up. His wife watches soberly from the other side of the bed. Cut to Jack and his wife dressed for work. His wife sees Jack wandering aimlessly around the house, turns and goes outside to the garden. She comes back with a single red rose and lays it on a counter in an alcove. The camera follows her to the kitchen, where Jack plays with a lighter and candle in the kitchen. But before the camera turns, we catch a brief glimpse of what looks like a photo and framed plaque in the alcove. With the rose lying in front of it, it has the appearance of a shrine. The photo may be of R. L. Adult Jack is played by Sean Penn, who was born in 1960. If we assume that Jack is several years older than R. L., then Jack was in his early twenties when his brother died at nineteen. Thirty years later, he still has trouble getting out of bed. "Why? Where were you?" The questions have never been answered, and he has not yet reconciled himself to that absence of answers.

Jack sleepwalks through work. He lives his life more by nature than grace. He complains about the degeneration of the world, and we hear his cynical comments about career and work to someone on the telephone. He is surrounded by natural men. A colleague tells him that he has broken up with a girlfriend or wife. "What are you going to do?" Jack asks. "Experiment" is the answer. In their glass tower, where the glory might shine through everywhere, Jack and his colleagues find reasons to be unhappy and ignore love smiling through everything. They walk in the way of nature.

As in the childhood scenes, language is a motif in the scenes of Jack's work day. Language—rather, the lack of it. He never exchanges words with his lovely wife. They don't even look at each other. She seems to understand and sympathize, but there is a barrier she cannot pass through. They live in a glass house, everything transparent, but they are utterly closed to one another. No real conversation goes on at work either. We hear a few fragments of business meetings, but everyone mumbles. As one analyst of the film says:

> Words are everywhere, but they are meaningless. An architect, he is also an activating Creator, and Malick makes us wonder about creation in all of its forms here in downtown Houston as both interiors (like elevators) and exteriors (looking up at the great skyscrapers) are photographed with wide angle lenses. It is streamlined to perfection, beautiful in its own way . . . but also denotes disconnection between beings, groundlessness, greed, and estrangement from anything Eternal: it is merely an omnipresent Now of isolated moments, just as it is filled with isolated words and isolated people. Beings are imprisoned by Time. The biblical connotation is to the Tower of Babel, where architectural genius elevated humankind to the height of God, but resulted in a confusion of language. . . . As in Babel, words go nowhere.[1]

As Jack ascends in an elevator while talking on the phone to his father, he apologizes for something he has said. He apparently blames his father for R. L.'s death. When language is used, it's as likely to harm as to help. He apologizes, and then adds, "It's just this day." He pauses to listen to his father, then responds, "Yeah. I think about him all the time." It's subtle, but now we know. Jack doesn't have trouble getting out of bed every day. It's just "this day," the anniversary of his brother's death. This day brings back a flood of memories, reawakens his sorrow, leaves him unsure whether life is worth living. It leaves him questioning the universe. Is this a world where the graced never come to a bad end? If it is, shouldn't we just turn in our ticket?

Jack's childhood memories are one of the wonders of the film. After Jack swims out of his womb/room into the world, Malick gives us ten minutes of momentary episodes in Jack's life. They are among the most charming moments in the film:

1. "Terrence Malick's Song of Himself," http://nilesfilmfiles.blogspot.com/2011/06/song-of-himself-terrence-malicks-tree.html.

- There is a closeup of Jack's infant face, fat cheek pressed against his mother's shoulder.
- Jack sucks his thumb while Mrs. O'Brien gazes at him rapturously and sings.
- Jack's baptism.
- Jack as a toddler giggling as he chases a ball around the dining room.
- Mr. O'Brien's feet and legs, with toddler Jack's in between, as he teaches Jack to walk.
- Mr. O'Brien shows Jack a flowering tree.
- Mrs. O'Brien reads to Jack, swings him round and round and round, shows him the scenes on a piece of decorated china.
- Mr. O'Brien tells a friend of the time when Jack bit the commander on the ankle during dinner.
- Jack's grandmother pulls the goldfish from the fishbowl to show him.
- A middle-aged man entertains Jack with mime.
- A worried Jack watches as his mother dab iodine on his injured foot and gently blows.
- Jack and his mother play with the mirror.
- Mrs. O'Brien catches a butterfly in flight and pets its wings on the ground.
- Jack bangs his rattle while Mrs. O'Brien dances in circles.
- Jack plays with his Noah's ark on the front law with his mother.
- R. L. is in a crib by the window, and toddler Jack enters from the left of the screen, wondering about this addition to his world.
- Jack leans in close to look at R. L., held in Mrs. O'Brien's arms. R. L. jerks his arm, accidentally hitting his older brother in the face. Jack responds with a "Huh!"
- Jack throws a tantrum in the yard, tossing one of his Noah's ark animals and threatening to throw another at his mother.
- Jack plays with bubbles in the yard.
- A man has a fit on the lawn as Mrs. O'Brien hurries Jack away, covering his eyes.

- Jack stubbornly asks for a piece of cake from his grandmother: "It's mine!"

- Jack plays hide and seek with his mother at the window.

- Jack helps his father plant and water the tree.

- Jack takes a bubble bath with R. L.

- Jack dresses up for Halloween.

- Mrs. O'Brien reads *Peter Rabbit* to Jack.

- Mrs. O'Brien swings Jack in circles, then points to the sky and says, "That's where God lives."

- Mr. O'Brien lights sparklers for everyone in the front yard.

- A leathery old man says, "Goodbye. We'll see you in five years."

- Jack or R. L. bounces on the bed, clapping arythmically.

- Mrs. O'Brien tickles Jack in the bed.

These scenes stay in the memory not only for their vivid depiction of infancy and childhood, but for their pacing. It is a montage, but it isn't rushed. The longest of the scenes lasts less than a minute, but during those seconds we share Mr. O'Brien's wonder at the feet of an infant, feel the sweet uncertainty of an older brother adjusting to a sibling, remember our own mother daubing a cut with iodine and blowing gently to cool it.

Jack is burdened with memories. That is the tragedy of his condition at the beginning of the film. Paradoxically, memory will be Jack's healer. Near the end of the scenes of Jack at work, he looks down the hallway and sees R. L. standing on a beach with sea foaming around his feet. "Find me," R. L. says. We know from the opening voice-overs that Mrs. O'Brien and R. L. were the ones who first led Jack to God's door. Jack has lost R. L., and has so lost God, lost his contact with the way of grace. He has also lost himself, lost his earlier more innocent, more living self. R. L. is somehow still there, still beckoning. Remembering R. L. is the way back to where he came from and can reunite the adult Jack with the teenage Jack. Moving back to find R. L. means moving back to join past and present so that he can face the future.

That vision of R. L. sets off the action of the rest of the film. The entire second half consists of Jack's memories of his childhood and boyhood. Jack's remembers his mother reading *The Jungle Book* and telling of the time she flew in an airplane. He remembers his father trying to teach him to box, and shards of his father's worldly wisdom. He remembers working at the weeds in the yard. He remembers his father returning from an over-seas trip, full of stories and gifts, and he remembers his father flirting with the waitress at the local diner. He remembers playing kickball at school, swinging on the rope and climbing the tree ladder, playing baseball with a football, and a dodge ball game that spread out over the whole yard round the house. He remembers running and biking in the cloud of DDT coming out of an insecticide truck, remembers playing in the fields and woods, pretending to find a dinosaur bone. He remembers attaching baseball cards to the back tire of his bike so it would sound like a motorcycle as he rode. He remembers the crush he had on a girl at school and conflicts with his father. Malick's own memory of 1950s boyhood is vivid. Anyone who grew up in the era recognizes scene after scene.[2]

Malick seems close to the edge of sentimentalism and pop psycho-logical schlock. Can memories really heal memories? It's worth noting that Jack's memories focus above all on R. L. and even more specifically on a se-ries of events at a particular time in their childhood. The hinge of his story is the drowning death of the boy in the town swimming pool, after which he embarks on a period of adolescent rebellion that climaxes in an act that harms his beloved brother, R. L. R. L. forgives him, and their reconciliation spills out in reconciliation with his father, a chastened man after losing his job at the plant. Memory leads back to God's door, but not just *any* memory. What takes him back is memory of his mother's way of grace, memory of his own evils, memory finally of his brother's grace and forgiveness. These are the memories that bring him back to the garden, to taste again of the tree of life. Malick may also have Jesus's parable of the prodigal son in mind. Jack is the wandering prodigal, far from his father's house, snuffling among the rubbish for food, when he remembers his father's house and begins his journey of return.

It's also worth noting that Jack's memories of R. L. are set within a panorama of cosmic scope, running from creation to eternal reunion. It's not the memory of R. L. per se that heals, but the memory of R. L. as one through whom the glory smiled, the glory of the Creator, the glory of the

2. Joe McCulloch goes so far as to suggest that Malick is attempting to provide a mythic portrait of "that idealized 50s life of romping boys and barking dogs and earthy country scenes," to provide "emotive and metaphysical underpinnings" to American boyhood ("Terrence Malick's 'The Tree of Life': A Few Thoughts Subsequence to a Local Screening Sponsored by a College's Theology Department," http://mubi.com/notebook/posts/terrence-malicks-the-tree-of-life-a-few-thoughts-subsequent-to-a-local-screen-ing-sponsored-by-a-colleges-theology-department).

world to come. Jack's memories are healed by penetrating back to the beginning of all beginnings, and when they are joined with hope for the end beyond all endings. Memory heals when it leads back to the flame that is Alpha and Omega.

Chapter 11

Family Table

"She only loves *me!*"

—Jack O'Brien

Jack is named in the film, but no one else is. We never learn Mr. or Mrs. O'Brien's first names, and we know their last names only from the credits. When Mrs. O'Brien calls the boys home from the front porch, she shouts out "Boys!" It's Jack's film, and he never called his parents by their first names. Their namelessness is also a sign of the estrangement within the family. Mr. O'Brien addresses Jack by his position, his "office," as "son"— "Son, fetch me my lighter"—just as he wants Jack to address him not by the familiar "Dad" but by the formal title "Father."

At the same time, this gives the family a mythic stature. They are an archetypal everyfamily, and that adds to the discomfort we feel as the family story unfolds before us. Through Jack's twelfth year, there is palpable tension between Mr. and Mrs. O'Brien, burning hostility that grows to murderous hatred between Jack and Mr. O'Brien, and even intensifying strife between the brothers. Alexander Desplat's static score holds our tension. We expect something to explode horrifically.

Welcome to the Freudian family.

The strains within the O'Brien family are especially evident at the dinner table. Family dinner is a American custom, representing hearth and home and all the virtues of Victorian, or 1950s, domesticity. In all cultures, meals taken together are occasions of communion. As each eats from a common table, sometimes from a common loaf or a common roast, they are bound together as one. We are one body because we partake of one loaf,

Paul told the Corinthians, but the same principle applies to meals other than the Eucharist.

The table scenes are the only scenes when the entire family is together. It is not a happy table. It is a place of un-communion, and Mr. O'Brien prevents conversation by forcefully expressing his own opinions and controlling the speech of the rest of the family. We see a brief glimpse of the family gathering during the opening discourse on nature and grace. A breeze is blowing into the house, fluttering the curtains. Mr. O'Brien prays to open the meal, and we move quickly on to another scene. In the first extended dinner scene, the strife simmers below the surface. Mr. O'Brien is demanding, looking for something to criticize. Jack asks for something, politely saying "please," but Mr. O'Brien isn't satisfied: "Please, sir!" he corrects. He asks Jack if he put the runners in the yard, and when Jack answers yes, Mr. O'Brien responds, "It didn't look like it." Jack looks slant-wise up at his father as he struggles to get a piece of meatloaf off the serving plate. Mrs. O'Brien breaks the silence by trying to tell her husband about Jack's book report. The teacher liked it, but Mr. O'Brien cuts her off before she can finish. He's listening to the Brahms symphony playing on his phonograph, and he gets up from the table to show off the record sleeve and announce "Brahms!"

The second dinner scene is worse. Mrs. O'Brien says nothing, but her eyes express a combination of reproach and fear. Mr. O'Brien is already unhappy when he sits down at the table. Jack has again failed to accomplish his chores in the yard, and Mr. O'Brien throws his napkin into his lap. At another dinner, Steve snickers at something and Mr. O'Brien sends him from the table. Jack smiles, and Mr. O'Brien asks if he wants to leave too. Jack says "No," and Mr. O'Brien immediately responds, "You're interrupting me. Am I finished? May I finish?" Jack nods, and Mr. O'Brien answers with a sarcastic "Thank you, your highness." Mrs. O'Brien lays a sympathetic hand on Jack's shoulder, but says nothing.

The climactic clash comes at the last supper. Mr. O'Brien is again a belligerent bully, and again the eruption has to do with his determination to control language. Holding a piece of rock, he demands of Jack, who sits beside him, "Did you actually pay Mr. Ledbetter for this? Don't say anything, just nod." From across the table, R. L. says, quietly but distinctly, "Be quiet." Shocked, Mr. O'Brien turns furiously and demands, "What did you say?" After a moment of silence, R. L. adds "Please." Everyone is suddenly in motion. Mr. O'Brien lunges across the table to grab R. L. Jack jumps up to pull his father back, "Leave him alone!" he screams. Mr. O'Brien carries

Jack and pushes him into a closet, closing the door. He returns to the table, where Mrs. O'Brien is holding Steve and trying to project R. L. Mr. O'Brien reaches past her, grabs R. L., and drags him out of the house. When he comes back to the table, he violently pulls the table straight and breathlessly continues his dinner, alone. Mrs. O'Brien leaves the room. "You turn my own kids against me," Mr. O'Brien tells his wife in the kitchen later. "You undermine everything I do." Mr. and Mrs. O'Brien have a scuffle in the kitchen when Mrs. O'Brien tries to wipe her husband's mouth with a dishrag, saying "How would you like it . . ." She never finishes the sentence, as her husband grabs her arms and twists her into submission.

After that battle, we never again see the O'Briens gathering for a family dinner. The dinner table appears several times. Sometimes Mr. O'Brien is at the table with a stack of folders and papers, working. At other times, he and his wife both stalk around the table, exchanging heated words. In frustration, Mr. O'Brien shoves a chair under the table. Once we see Mr. O'Brien eating at the table, but he's by himself.

Mr. O'Brien lives by nature, and this produces a host of vices that are obvious to young Jack. He is a hypocrite, insisting that the boys not put their elbows on the table even as he does and making Jack close the screen door quietly when he bursts through it like a cannonball. He is a failure but cannot admit it to himself, so he lies and makes up stories of triumph. He tells his children not to interrupt, but he interrupts his wife and boys constantly, rarely listening when they try to tell him something. "Why does he hurt us?" Jack asks, apparently in a prayer. Jack recognizes all this and grows to hate his father. At one point, Jack goes so far as to pray for his father's death. In a wrenching scene that seems to go on forever, Jack walks around the back of a jacked-up car underneath which his father is working. He gazes at the jack, ready to give it a kick and let the car fall on top of his father.

Much of Jack's hatred for his father comes from his father's petty cruelties and abuse. But there is also a level of rivalry for Mrs. O'Brien. Jack's sexual awakening is initially focused on a girl in his class, Samantha. He flirts with her at school, using some of the playful tricks he learned from his father, and he follows her home from school, walking at a creepy distance. But that attraction soon gets projected elsewhere. Chasing a ball down the street, he watches through a window as a family drama unfolds in a neighbor's house, the Kimballs, the wealthy family that is able to keep a yard man and has growing grass because they have money. Mr. Kimball, drunk, screams at his wife, "This is my house! I let you stay here." Later, Jack sees the woman through the window in a dress, and then passing by the window wearing a slip. He watches her through the window of her turret room, watches her hanging the laundry on the clothesline, her body silhouetted behind a sheet. The camera focuses in as she rinses grass cuttings from her feet with the garden hose, and we know we are watching through Jack's hungry eyes. She modestly raises her dress to wash her calves, and then offers a drink to Jack from the same hose.

Sometimes a hose is just a hose; sometimes a staircase is just a staircase. Stairs are ladders to heaven, mystical mediators of ascent, but Malick knows Freud well enough to know that staircases are a common Freudian image of sexual excitement leading to climax.

> Steep inclines, ladders, and stairs, and going up or down them, are symbolic representations of the sexual act. Smooth walls over which one climbs, facades of houses, across which one lets oneself down—often with a sense of great anxiety—correspond to erect human bodies, and probably repeat in our dreams childish memories of climbing up parents or nurses. "Smooth" walls are men; in anxiety dreams one often holds firmly to 'projections' on houses. Tables, whether bare or covered, and boards, are women, perhaps by virtue of contrast, since they have no protruding contours.[1]

Malick shows us staircase after staircase. Toddler Jack looks up a staircase toward a light, and opens a door to look up the staircase to the attic. Adolescent Jack climbs over fences, and climbs steps to Mrs. Kimball's dressing table.

Jack's attraction to Samatha and Mrs. Kimball is confusingly mixed with sexual attraction to his mother. Especially when Mr. O'Brien leaves for an extended international business trip, Jack begins to watch his mother closely. He watches her cooling herself in a sprinkler, her dress clinging to her. She moves from room to room in a sheer night gown, fixing her hair and getting ready for the day. Jack wanders outside in the hall outside stealing glances. If that were not obvious enough, when Mr. O'Brien returns from his trip, Jack savagely confronts him in the back yard. "She only loves *me!*" he screams.

Malick may have some general commitment to Freudian theory, but in the film the Freudian resonances have a more specific genesis. Jack becomes estranged from his father because of his father's own foolishness. As Mr. O'Brien says late in the film, he wanted to become a great man, a big

---

1. Freud, *Interpretation of Dreams* (New York: Macmillan, 1913), 676.

man, wanted to be loved for his achievements. This led only to shame, and after losing his job he realizes that he dishonored the glory. The world is full of beauties that he never saw because he was so intent on putting his imprint on the world. Living in the way of nature invites rivalries and combat.

The family table is ultimately restored to something like its former use. When Mr. O'Brien returns home with the news that the plant has closed and he is losing his job, Mrs. O'Brien is holding flowers to adorn the table. For the first time since the fight, we see both of them sitting at the table. We watch from the yard, through the dining room window. Mr. O'Brien has been humbled, his wife takes his hands in a gesture of forgiveness and reconciliation, and a breeze blows from inside the house, billowing the curtains out the window. Humbled, Mr. O'Brien has been opened up to glory, and the glory is streaming in.

Chapter 12

Death and Sin

"I can't do what I want. What I do I hate."

—JACK O'BRIEN

THE TREE OF LIFE is centrally concerned with what philosophers and theologians know as the problem of evil: How do we account for suffering? How could a good and omnipotent God create a world where true and kind boys like R. L. die prematurely? If boys like R. L. die randomly, perhaps there is no God, or perhaps he is not good, or perhaps he's just too weak to do anything about it.

Death, especially premature death, poses these questions. Despite sentimental distortions, Christianity treats death as an enemy. Death is an unwelcome, acidic intrusion into the world, following on the heels of the sin of the one man (Rom 5:12) and spreading until everything comes under its rule. It is the "last enemy" (1 Cor 15). For the writer to the Hebrews, men are in slavery throughout their lives because of the fear of death (2:15). In the biblical wisdom literature, especially in Ecclesiastes, death is the solvent of human achievement, the great leveler. Human beings are created with eternity in their hearts, with an aspiration toward immortality, but death turns human beings into nothing but vapor. And because human beings are vapor, smoke, and mist, so are all their achievements. The pain Solomon feels when he surveys the world is the pain of knowing that, no matter what he makes of life, he will die and have to leave it to those that follow after. "Vapor of vapors," he observes. "All is vapor."

We live in a world of shadows, and those shadows are ourselves. "Our days on earth are as a shadow," Job says (8:9), and when they are done a "land of darkness and deep shadow" awaits (10:21). Man is no more than a breath, like a passing shadow (Ps 144:4). Death casts it shadow into the most sunlit lives (Pss 44:19; 107:10, 14), and everyone who has ever lived has had to pass through the valley of the shadow of death.

The world of *The Tree of Life* is a world of shadows. In an arresting shot early in the film, Malick turns the camera upside down to watch children playing on a road or driveway. We can barely see the children's feet at the top of the screen, and the shot is filled with their shadows extending downward playing games on what looks like the surface of the sky. We see the shadow of the delivery boy carrying the news of R. L.'s death approaching the O'Brien's door before we see the delivery boy. In one scene, Jack dances up and down the front steps of the house, but the camera pays closer attention to the shadow he casts on the steps. This world and all who live in it are like passing shadows that strut and fret our hour. Death will eventually catch up with us, and our shadowy existence will be swallowed up into the shadow of death.

Mr. O'Brien thinks that death can be handled, managed, and controlled like everything else. After R. L.'s funeral, still dressed up, he's back to the yard work, holding the hose and trying to get his grass to grow. One of Mrs. O'Brien's friends lingers, and he shoos her away: "Go on, now. We're all right." Death comes, but it's all part of life, nothing to go on about. When a boy drowns at the local swimming pool, Mr. O'Brien jumps into action. He is always directing traffic, telling one boy to go here and a man to go there. He tries to revive the boy with mouth-to-mouth resuscitation. Mr. O'Brien is the kind of man you want nearby in an emergency. Nothing ruffles him. He is always in control, even of death. Mrs. O'Brien's mother, trying to comfort her after R. L.'s death, has a similar attitude. "Things change," she offers. "You'll get over it in time."

Mrs. O'Brien doesn't want to get over it. She doesn't want the wound to heal. This might be morbidity on her part, a determination to wallow in sorrow, but I take it as something else. Mrs. O'Brien is undone by the death of her favorite son. Death challenges her confidence in God, her faith that there is order and meaning and justice in the universe. Death assaults her commitment to be "true . . . whatever comes." She feels R. L.'s death as her own, as the death of the world, as a tear in the fabric of things, and she doesn't respond to this rend in the universe with a "We're OK. Go on, now. We're all right." The air around the O'Brien home fills with shrieks, all the more haunting because they are disembodied, sourceless. It's as if the trees, the earth itself, were groaning for her children. Her tears and cries rise up all the way to heaven, and fill space as far as any telescope can see. Precisely because she walks the way of grace, seeing the glory shining through everything, she becomes fragile in the face of death.

Jack feels the weight of death in the way that his mother does. When the boy drowns in the swimming pool, he wonders how God could have let that happen. "Where were you?" he asks, and he wonders why he should be good if God is not. He wonders if the boy died because he was bad. That would make sense of things. But a boy dying who did not seem to deserve any such thing—Jack finds that intolerable.

The film presents us with Mr. O'Brien's natural response to death, an inhuman, businesslike Stoicism, and alongside it Mrs. O'Brien's paralysis of unending grief. Is there any third way? Is it possible for time to lessen the sting of loss without accommodating to the enemy?

The Christian answer to this dilemma centers on the cross, where death is overcome by death. Though Malick's film is not explicitly evangelical, the answer it gives is consistent with the Christian answer. Death is an enemy, and if death is not finally overcome, then the only proper response to the world is an endless shriek, unending tears. If what is lost can never be recovered, if death is *forever*, then the world truly is meaningless. But the film makes it clear that there is life, and reunion, beyond the grave. Jack finds R. L. again, standing on the beach, and in one of the most moving moments of the film, Mrs. O'Brien finds R. L. too, her face radiant with the terrible shock of joy. Like Abraham, she can give up her son because she knows that she is not giving him up. He has simply gone ahead, and will be waiting for her when she arrives. She already knows this from the beginning in a confused way. She longs for death: "I just want to die, so I can be with him," she tells her husband. That will not do. She has to wait, but wait in hope of a future reunion, a restoration on the beach beside an infinite ocean.

Perhaps the film's best answer to the dilemma of death is the scene that follows the funeral for the drowned boy. The three O'Brien boys are in the cemetery, balancing on the walls, leaping from grave to grave. Jack hides behind a gravestone, and jumps out to scare his youngest brother, Steve. They chase one another through the cemetery. Can you play in a graveyard? Earth is a graveyard of the species that have come and gone. From Malick's viewpoint, it is packed with the castoffs from the process of natural selection. And it is a graveyard for all the human beings that have gone before. If we cannot dance with shadows, we will never dance. If we can never see the glory shining there, we will find it nowhere. Can you dance on a grave? We had better be able to, because the cemetery of the world is the only dance floor we have.

Malick is at his most profound in exposing the connections between the problem of evil and inexplicable suffering and the reality of human sin. Sin is not the same as evil. In the Bible, "sin" is used in a number of different senses. It refers to particular acts of disobedience to God's commandments. Committing adultery is a sin, as is murder and theft. Sinners commit *sins*. But the apostle Paul rarely uses the word "sin" in the plural. In the singular it does not refer to particular actions but to a dominating and enslaving power that controls a person to such an extent that he finds himself incapable of acting well. Romans 7 is one of the classic passages in the New Testament about the dominating power of sin:

> For we know that the Law is spiritual, but I am of flesh, sold into bondage to sin. For what I am doing, I do not understand; for I am not practicing what I would like to do, but I am doing the very thing I hate. But if I do the very thing I do not want to do, I agree with the Law, confessing that the Law is good. So now, no longer am I the one doing it, but sin which dwells in me. For I know that nothing good dwells in me, that is, in my flesh; for the willing is present in me, but the doing of the good is not. For the good that I want, I do not do, but I practice the very evil that I do not want. But if I am doing the very thing I do not want, I am no longer the one doing it, but sin which dwells in me (vv. 14–20).[1]

Sin causes evil actions, but it is not the evil actions themselves. It is a force, a power that enslaves.

One of the phrases for sin in Leviticus, often translated as "sin of inadvertency" is closely related to the Hebrew verb for "wander." It is a sin of "going astray" or "wandering" (e.g., Lev 4:2). Sinners are prodigals, wandering through life. Along similar lines, Orthodox theologians emphasize that sin is essentially not actions but estrangement from God. The Russian Orthodox theologian Alexander Schmemann wrote that "The world is a fallen world because it has fallen away from the awareness that God is all in all. The accumulation of this disregard for God is the original sin that

---

1. This is a more complex passage than it might appear. In the context of Romans, it has to do mainly with the way sin coopts something good—the law of God—and turns it into an instrument of death. In the end, Paul seems to exonerate the "I" from responsibility. It is "sin" that does the evil, not the "I."

blights the world." For Schmemann, sin is not fundamentally disobedience, and certainly not a neglect of "religious duties." Rather, man's sin "is that he ceased to be hungry for Him and Him alone, ceased to see his whole life as a sacrament of communion with God."[2]

Something like this understanding of sin is evident in the film, when Jack questions how he lost contact with the God who knew him before he knew God. "When did I wander from you?" Jack asks. As the film begins, Jack reconstructs the process by which he became estranged from God. It begins with the drowning of a friend in the community swimming pool. "Where were you," Jack asks in challenge to God. "You let a boy die." In the next frames we see the scarred head and stringy hair of a boy who had been burned in a fire. "You let anything happen," Jack concludes. The problem of evil raises a question not about God's *existence* but about his *goodness*. Jack does not leave the question at that philosophical level. If God is not good, then how can God demand goodness of his creatures? Is God as much of a hypocrite as Mr. O'Brien? If he lets anything happen, why can't people do what *they* want? "Why should I be good when you're not?" Jack wants to know. It is a revised version of Ivan Karamazov's syllogism: Not, "If there is no God, all is permitted" but "If God is not *good*, all is permitted."

When Mr. O'Brien leaves for a business trip, Jack and his brothers are initially exuberant. They run through the house whooping like Indians, frightening their mother with a lizard. Jack mockingly screams out some of his father's instructions: *"Don't slam the screen door!"* They spend an idyllic afternoon on a picnic with their mother. Tight bonds are loosed and they are able to breathe free in the realm of grace. But estrangement doesn't remain still, and in his father's absence Jack begins a descent into a preadolescent hell on a path of low-level juvenile delinquency. He breaks out the windows of a neighbor's garage. He and his friends blow up bird eggs with firecrackers, and launch a frog attached to a bottle rocket. Jack becomes a ring-leader of the gang, but he is taunted to his worst sins by another boy, a tempter. The sequence of events in this section of the film is critical:

- Boy drowns.
- Fight at the dinner table.
- Mr. O'Brien leaves for a business trip.
- Jack begins to peek into the Kimball's windows.

2. Schmemann, *For the Life of the World: Sacraments and Orthodoxy* (Crestwood, NY: St. Vladimir's Seminary Press, 1973), 17–18.

- Jack joins his friends in destroying bird eggs and frogs.

- Taunted by his friend, Jack sneaks into the Kimball house.

- Jack acts cruelly toward R. L.

Jack's is a graduated estrangement from his family. It begins with hostility to his father. Jack thinks his father hypocritical, boastful, a liar. He comes at one point to wish so intensely for his father's death that he asks God to kill Mr. O'Brien. It spreads to estrangement from his mother. Jack recognizes early in the film that his mother and brother led him to God's door. When he begins to question God's goodness, he is gradually estranged from the people closest to him too. She scolds him for one of his pranks, and he screams at her through the screen door: "You can't tell me what to do!" But his transgression of the Kimball's house sets up the most impenetrable barrier between himself as his mother:

> [The Kimballs'] door is unlocked. He invades the space, finally on the other side of the frame (before, he was always peering through those windows and doorways). He sees the window curtains blowing above air vents: this is the house belonging to the family that Jack's father envies and resents, who can evidently afford air conditioning, in addition to a pristine lawn. Jack passes through a hallway (where we see a birdcage in a room) and then enters the woman's dressing room. He looks at a mirror and holds her earrings. . . . Jack takes [her slip] out of a drawer and lays it on the bed, staring at it, imagining. Malick does not show us what Jack does next, but . . . we should believe that he has masturbated over the slip. . . . The close-up on his face as he intensely *gazes* at the slip cuts to him running in a sweat by the riverside with the slip. At first he hides it beneath a piece of wood. But then he lets it flow down the river. He goes home and cannot look at his mother or talk to her. The feminine ideal and attachment has been transmuted to the flowing River of Life.[3]

On the way back from the river, Jack breaks his stick against a tree, then throws it into a yard. For the Freudian side of Malick, it's a phallic symbol; to the biblical side of Malick it is a sign that he has lost his connection to the tree of life. Innocence evaporates with his sexual transgression. He flails against the tree of life, and once he throws his stick away he's no longer part of a tree of life himself.

3. "Terrence Malick's Song of Himself V—the Tree of Life: Los Demiurgos," http://nilesfilmfiles.blogspot.com/2011/06/song-of-himself-terrence-malicks-tree.html.

When Jack gets home, his mother waits in the front yard, her arms firmly folded in front of her and her face firm with a cross scold. In the next scene, Jack leans against a tree, crying. A hand—Mrs. O'Brien's, we guess—wipes away a tear, but Jack doesn't want comfort. "I can't talk to you," he says. "Don't look at me." Thunder rolls in the background, the Lord walking in the garden in the cool of the day. Jack is Adam among the bushes hiding from God, Adam in his shame hiding from Eve, mother of all the living. Again the failure of language marks the estrangement. We suspect that we are seeing the birth of the adult Jack, the husband who can barely look at his wife, the architect who mumbles to his co-workers. "I can't talk to you. Don't look at me" becomes the theme of his adult life. Jack knows that he has crossed a line. "What have I started?" he asks himself. "What have I done?" On the screen, we see his mother covering him with a sheet and spinning him, laughing. She is still there, his mother of grace, but he is now a shadow behind a veil.

But the worst is yet to come. R. L. is Jack's most immediate guide to the presence of God. He is good and kind, brave enough to stand up to his father, compassionate. But after sin in the Kimballs' house and his estrangement from his mother, Jack begins to act with unmotivated hatred toward R. L. When he knocks a cup of water onto his brother's water painting, he storms out the screen door screaming at his mother. Tension grows between the brothers. Play-fighting in the yard turns serious. Jack convinces R. L. to put his finger into the socket of a lamp, and frightens his brother by pretending the lamp is plugged in. "Trust me," he says. R. L. does trust him, but he shouldn't. In the most shocking scene in the film, Jack persuades R. L. to put his finger over the end of a BB gun. This time, it's not pretend. The gun is loaded and Jack fires a BB into R. L.'s finger. Several times in the film the sound nearly goes dead and the dialogue and natural sounds are muffled. Early in the film, the sound of an airplane is muffled as Mr. O'Brien receives the news of R. L.'s death in a phone call. In the shooting scene, as soon as Jack fires, the sound muffles. It's as if we have gone slightly deaf. We can no longer hear the singing of birds or the crickets in the grass. The world that shines with glory goes silent for a time.

This is the depth of Jack's descent into evil. Breaking the neighbor's windows is mischievous. Hatred of his father is wicked, but we have learned enough about his father to understand why he would hate him. His hostility to his mother is less excusable, and is mostly a projection of hatred of his father onto his father's wife. But his abuse of R. L. is completely baseless.

It is, as Coleridge said of Shakespeare's Iago, "motiveless malignancy." It is evil for the sake of evil, cruelty for its own sake. Shooting his brother's finger gains Jack nothing. It doesn't even gain the admiration of his fellow ruffians. It is wholly gratuitous.

In the wake of the shooting, Jack finds that his desire for autonomy inverts. He murmurs defiantly to his mother, "I'm gonna do what I want." But after shooting R. L.'s finger, he admits to himself and to God that this is not his actual condition. Rather, he is in the condition of the "I" of Romans 7. "What I want to do I can't do. I do what I hate." He recognizes that his cruelty has taken him to a distant place, far from R. L. and therefore far from God. As he explores a broken-down house with his friends and swims under a waterfall, he wonders, "How can I get back to where they are?" He's been a wandering prodigal; now he is ready to head home. In the background of Jack's confession, we hear a few lines of *Lacrimosa* in solo piano. Earlier in the film, *Lacrimosa* provided musical expression of the anguished "Why?" in the face of death and pain. Here it is brought in to connect Jack's moral wandering with the problem of evil. The fact of creation is the Joban response to the intellectual and philosophical problem of evil. Now Jack looks for an answer to the moral problem of evil: How can I be freed from the body of this death?

Paul's answer to that question is explicitly Christological; Malick's is implicitly Christological. Jack begins to return to the God who knew him from the beginning when he is reconciled with R. L. Before an open window—with glory shining through—Jack offers R. L. a chance to take vengeance for the shot to his finger. Jack hands R. L. a long piece of wood and says, "You can hit me with this if you want." R. L. makes a few feints, but smiles. "I'm sorry," Jack says, "You're my brother." R. L. lays a hand on Jack's shoulder, the film's gesture of compassion, forgiveness, and reconnection. What creation is to the intellectual problem of evil, forgiveness is to the moral problem of evil. Forgiveness ends cycles of cruelty and sin.

All this occurs in the adult Jack's memory on "this day," the anniversary of R. L.'s death. Jack remembers wandering, transgressing, hurting his brother without cause. And he remembers his brother's forgiveness, his echo of Cordelia's great line to her offending father. Lear tells Cordelia, "Your sisters have, as I do remember, done me wrong: You have some cause, they have not." To which Cordelia instantly replies, "No cause, no cause." Adult Jack has been wondering the same thing that he wondered as an adolescent: "What have I started? How do I get back to where they are?" When

Jack remembers that moment of forgiveness, compassion, grace, when R. L. renounced vengeance and took his hand, he begins his journey back. He is ready to pass through the door in the desert and follow the sound of the waves to the water's edge.

Chapter 13

The Promised End

Ivan Karamazov knew it, as did Kierkegaard and the author of Job before them both: Every human loss, every pain, every undeserved tear, every act of malice puts a question mark over the cosmos. What kind of world is this where such things happen? If there is a God, what kind of God is this who allows such things, or, what seems worse, does more than allow? Might there perhaps be two gods, more or less equally powerful, locked in an eternal, inconclusive struggle for mastery? Every loss raises questions about where it all came from and where it is all going, about origins and destiny. Every moment of pain poses questions of creation and eschatology.

Whether or not Malick learned this from Job, in *The Tree of Life* he appeals to Job to make the point. Job is quoted at the beginning of the movie. There is a long church scene where the sermon is on Job. The O'Briens lose their son, the son of grace, as Job lost everything. R. L.'s death seems to put the lie to the nuns' Panglossian optimism about people in the way of grace, who are never supposed to come to a bad end. But the truth or falsity of the nuns' claim depends on what that end is. A quarter of the way through Job, and halfway, and nearly to the end, we are left thinking that Job, a blameless man, has come to a bad end and we with Job wonder about the justice of God. For the same reason, R. L.'s death raises the question of ultimate destiny, of the end of everything. If death is the end, then people who walk in the way of grace do come to senselessly bad ends. But for Job loss and suffering is *not* the end. Yahweh appears to him in a storm cloud, and at the very end not only restores what he has lost but restores it with interest. If we know the trajectory of the book of Job, we watch *The Tree of Life* waiting for resolutions. If loss has the final word, then we are watching a truncated book of Job, a story of a Job who disappears from the text before the encounter with Yahweh and before he gets everything returned. If Malick follows Job to the end, to the end of all ends at the end of time, we expect scenes of restoration.

We do, but they are understated. There is no storm cloud or divine voice. R. L. stays dead, and the O'Briens have no more children to replace him. But the film concludes first with fragmentary glimpses of resurrection and then a long sequence of reunion in eternity. Two statues lie in the grass, with what looks like a Middle Eastern town behind. Or perhaps they are corpses, already beginning to rise, still wrapped like mummies, soon to be walking. A woman dressed as a bride lies motionless in an old building, but then next moment we see her walking. Mrs. O'Brien stands at the top of a grave, extending her hand to pull someone from death, and a hand appears below to grasp hers.[1]

And then we come to a long scene of final reunion. Along an endless wave-beaten stretch of white beach, all the characters in the film (and, it seems, more) wander about. Jack's entire family is there, and so is the kid who got his hair singed in the house fire, and so is the girl that Jack once had a crush on. R. L. is there, smiling with a shy reticence as Mrs. O'Brien, her face

---

1. Malick filmed much more extensive scenes of resurrection that confirm his intention. According to a crew member, "At Reimer's [Ranch], there was staged a scene with thirteen extras playing the Rising Dead walking through the town carrying candles. At the nearby river, there were more dead emerging from the water and 'wet' souls receding into the same. There was also an angel with hands outstretched feeling the river. Some of the listed extras were 5 "young risen dead" and 1 "teen risen dead." I think it may have not been used because it may have been deemed too religious for the film. In the river scenes, there were special shoes with cameras on them to be used . . . The faces of the dead were smeared with ash. A special ladder and ramp were also set up and used in the film. . . . At the end of this day's filming, Malick staged a large scene in the courtyard of the San Antonia mission set which featured a number of dead souls with candles. Malick had extensive discussions during the day with key crew members while he tried to decide whether to use two- or three-wick candles. They ultimately decided on the three-wick candles. During this scene, the dead souls carried lit candles which they used to light the unlit candles of the other souls. Malick stood behind the Steadicam while they were filming, holding a lit candle that he would pass to the souls as their candles would go out. Chivo was not happy during the filming of this scene, as it was very close to sunset, and the lack of available light forced him to remove all the filters on the camera and open the lens wide open." Paul Maher, Jr., ed., *One Big Soul: An Oral History of Terrence Malick* (N.p.: Lulu, Kindle edition, 2012).

a shock of disbelief, stares at him and hugs him. Jack and R. L. embrace, as do Jack and his mother. Mr. and Mrs. O'Brien kiss for the first time in the film, and passionately. The entire action of the film is driven by Jack's vision of R. L. standing in the distance along this same beach, saying "Find me." Jack has found him, and finds himself and finds everyone else alongside.

It is, as one commentator has pointed out, the same beach where we have earlier seen a plesiosaur wounded in the side:

> Through the prism of Grace, the plesiosaur could be seen as a Christ reference—the *lapis* or Fish, an archetype of the deep unconscious (the ocean) with a gash on its side (like Christ crucified). In alchemy, the Fish is associated with Christ, and in Arthurian romance with the Fisher King, keeper of the Holy Grail. Finally, R. L., the suicide, is linked with Christ (who also, essentially, chose death) when at church he looks up at the stained-glass image of Jesus, his hands bounded, relating not only to Malick's recurring motifs of boundaries and cages that impede freedom, but also the hands his brother broke.[2]

Fittingly, the *Agnus Dei* from Berlioz's *Requiem* fills the soundscape. Some viewers have complained about the anemic "heaven" that closes the film. If this is heaven, it doesn't seem to be much to look forward to. The characters aren't zombies, but they might be as they walk deliberately and aimlessly up and down the beach. It's a lovely setting, the reunions are moving, and Berlioz's *Agnus Dei* deepens the scene immeasurably. But one hopes for more from an afterlife. Something like this:

> For behold, I create new heavens and a new earth; and the former things will not be remembered or come to mind. . . . No longer will there be in it an infant who lives but a few days, or an old man who does not live out his days; for the youth will die at the age of one hundred and the one who does not reach the age of one hundred will be thought accursed. They will build houses and inhabit them; they will also plant vineyards and eat their fruit. They will not build and another inhabit, they will not plant and another eat; for as the lifetime of a tree, so will be the days of My people,

---

2. "Terrence Malick's Song of Himself,"
http://nilesfilmfiles.blogspot.com/2011/06/song-of-himself-terrence-malicks-tree. html. The same essay points out that R. L. buries a fish in the yard behind the house as they get ready to move. Every Christian knows that buried fish don't stay buried. One clarification: In the film, R. L.'s death is unexplained. But R. L. is a fictionalized version of Malick's brother, who did commit suicide.

and My chosen ones will wear out the work of their hands. (Isa 65:17, 20–22)

Or this:

> Then I saw a new heaven and a new earth; for the first heaven and the first earth passed away, and there is no longer any sea. And I saw the holy city, new Jerusalem, coming down out of heaven from God, made ready as a bride adorned for her husband. . . . And he carried me away in the Spirit to a great and high mountain, and showed me the holy city, Jerusalem, coming down out of heaven from God, having the glory of God. Her brilliance was like a very costly stone, as a stone of crystal-clear jasper. . . . And the city has no need of the sun or of the moon to shine on it, for the glory of God has illumined it, and its lamp is the Lamb. The nations will walk by its light, and the kings of the earth will bring their glory into it. In the daytime (for there will be no night there) its gates will never be closed; and they will bring the glory and the honor of the nations into it; and nothing unclean, and no one who practices abomination and lying, shall ever come into it, but only those whose names are written in the Lamb's book of life. (Rev 21:1–2, 10–11, 23–27)

It would be a perfect vision to end Malick's movie because in scripture the tree of life comes back in abundance in this new urban Eden:

> Then he showed me a river of the water of life, clear as crystal, coming from the throne of God and of the Lamb, in the middle of its street. On either side of the river was the tree of life, bearing twelve kinds of fruit, yielding its fruit every month; and the leaves of the tree were for the healing of the nations. . . . And there will no longer be any night; and they will not have need of the light of a lamp nor the light of the sun, because the Lord God will illumine them; and they will reign forever and ever. (Rev 22:1–2, 5).

The biblical scenes of eternity are teeming with life, not only the life of human beings but the life of the creation. In Malick's eternity, the world as we know it is gone, obliterated (perhaps) by the same sort of astronomical catastrophe that gave us the run of the planet in the first place. For a film entitled *The Tree of Life*, it is shocking to end with a beach without a tree in sight.[3]

---

3. Insofar as the scene is biblically inspired at all (and it may not be), it owes more to the scenes at the edge of the heavenly ocean than to the scenes of the new Jerusalem: "And I saw, as it were, a sea of glass mixed with fire, and those who had come off victorious from the beast and from his image and from the number of his name, standing on

What we get instead is a scene of utter calm.[4] Berlioz swells on the soundtrack, but we hear no words. Language, so prominent a theme of the film, virtually drops away. People are moving, but they aren't going anywhere. Like the ocean they seem ready and willing to keep slapping against the waves aeon upon aeon. Jack's prayer seems to be literally fulfilled: "Guide us until the *end of time.*" This is a beach beyond and outside of time. That's one of the reasons we can see Jack as an adult, while the rest of his family remains the same age they have been throughout the film. Jack could be his mother's brother, or her lover, and we involuntarily feel a shudder of that old Freudian frisson.[5]

If this is Malick's vision of heaven or the new creation, the critics have a point: It's less than we hope for as an end to a cosmos that began with the grandeur and violence that Malick depicts in the evolution sequence. To think of this straightforwardly as "heaven" or as "new creation," however, may be asking too much. The inconsistency of Jack as an adult when no one else has aged gives us a clue. This is not heaven, but Jack completing his journey to find his younger self and especially to reunite with R. L. It is a vision of a future reconciliation of everyone and everything, but it is only a glimpse. It's the end of all things glimpsed momentarily and through a glass darkly.

A second key to the scene has to do with Mrs. O'Brien. Jack asks early in the movie how she was able to cope with R. L.'s death. How did she survive the loss? He doesn't know, and neither do we until toward the end. Mrs. O'Brien, flanked by two women to form a circle of the three graces, releases R. L. to God. "I give him to you." This must have happened before the end of all things. Finding R. L., Jack realizes that his mother coped by offering her son to God in faith, a faith that included hope that she would see him again.

Having glimpsed the promised end, Jack imitates his mother. After the long beach scene, we see Jack walk out from the glass office building that does more to deflect the glory than to admit it. He takes a deep breath, looks up, and for the first time his face relaxes into what for Sean Penn must pass for a smile. Jack has found R. L., and now he can give him into

---

the sea of glass holding harps of God, and they sang the song of Moses the bond-servant of God and the song of the Lamb" (Rev 15:2–3).

4. This point is emphasized in "Terrence Malick's Song of Himself," http://nilesfilmfiles. blogspot.com/2011/06/song-of-himself-terrence-malicks-tree.html

5. Common as this idea is, I don't think timelessness is a Christian vision of eternity. Human beings are created temporal, and so long as we are human we will remain temporal. And we will be human forever, never growing to become some sort of trans-human species.

the hands of God. He has rediscovered the lesson R. L. taught him so long ago, and he can be reconciled to the universe. The requiem that is the film comes to an end. As the Anglican *Book of Common Prayer* funeral service says, "In sure and certain hope of the resurrection to eternal life . . . we commend to Almighty God our brother . . . and we commit his body to the ground." The act of committal by both Mrs. O'Brien and Jack is rooted in their restored confidence in the order of the universe. Knowing that R. L.'s death at nineteen is *not* his end, Mrs. O'Brien and Jack can trust the nuns. Those who live in the way of grace may die young. They may die horribly. But they never come to a bad *end* because death is not the end. We are quite a ways beyond Heidegger here. Whatever other influence he had on Malick's vision, Malick doesn't accept that death is the limit, that time has a final horizon beyond which the rest is silence. Beyond death there is reconciliation, reunion, hope.

Beyond death, there are sunflowers. The sunflower is a perfect image for the way of grace. Its name is suggestive of heavenly glory. In color and shape, it is a reflex of the burning suns of what might be an infinite universe. Malick uses Hubble Telescope pictures of deep space, but one doesn't have to have a telescope to see the glory shine. Suns grow in the backyard, if we our eyes are open windows. Sunflowers follow the sun through the day, the perfect botanical expression of the way of grace that receives the glory. It's the perfect Heideggerian flower that never forgets Being. But Malick does something stunning with his sunflowers. The first shot of is a close-up of a single flower, as Mrs. O'Brien speaks of the way of grace. We can see others dancing in the wind behind, but we concentrate on this one. At the end of the film, the camera pulls back, a brilliant blue sky fills the top two-thirds of the screen, and we see a breathtaking field of sunflowers. Through the suffering and loss that the movie depicts, the single sunflower of grace blossoms into a field of sunflowers. It's Job, surrounded by his second family that he can love. It's *Brothers Karamazov*. It's the Agnus Dei and all seeds that go into the earth to die, so they can produce fruit.

The very last visual in the movie is a lingering shot of a suspension bridge. The sound of lapping water that began the movie closes the movie. We have been on the beach all the time, with the entire tumultuous drama of the O'Brien family circumscribed by the hope of reunion. The sea is as much an alpha and omega as the flame of God himself. But the bridge is new. As trees link earth to the sky where God lives, as ladders are places where angels ascend and descend, so bridges link beginnings with endings, the past and the eternal future. As the film is a branching tree, so the film is a bridge, linking us all to the beginnings of all things, pointing us to the ends of all things and suspending our every loss lovingly between.

As we gaze at the bridge, a lone gull swoops past, curving gracefully and exiting screen right. The Spirit hovering over the waters? The dove descending on Jesus? The dove that tells Noah the flood is over and the world is cleansed? It is all that and more, for the glimpse of the promised end renews Jack's hope for a future reunion, across the bridge of time, in a world made new by the hovering Spirit.

Made in the USA
Lexington, KY
15 December 2015